# What is
# GOD SAYING?

*And Other Lessons from a Spiritual Father*

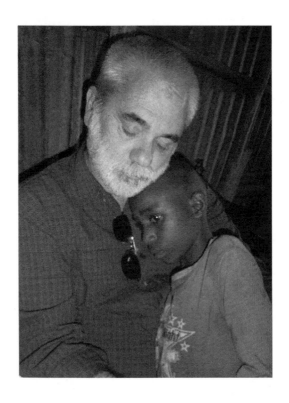

*by*

**Randy Conger**

# What is God Saying?

## and other Lessons from a Spiritual Father

# Dedication

My wife Jodene, my children; Charity, Tiffanie, Grace and Stephen, and to all those who have allowed me the honor to speak into their lives. I love you all.

# Special Thanks

To Annie Korkeakoski-Sears, Christina Zeeb, David Hazel, Emily Henderson, Julie Smith, Roger Shipman and Marilyn Lorance for the long and painful effort of editing this book. My appreciation for your effort and sacrifice exceed the words I have to express.

# What others are saying....

Randy, my friend for over 40 years, has written an astoundingly helpful and accessible book that will inspire and renew confidence in the God of the impossible. If you want a life of adventure and want to become like Jesus this is for you.

The miracles in this book at times stagger the imagination. Nevertheless, Randy does much more than recount miracle stories. He powerfully awakens our hearts to the transforming love of Christ available to everyone.

Like a loving father, Randy freely shares insights and understanding gained over four decades of pioneering ministry. This book is a veritable treasure trove of wisdom in how to navigate a supernatural life and remain grounded and loving. If Randy is anything, he is authentic!

This is the genuine instructive adventure story of a man who has learned to walk in intimacy with God. Randy's credentials include countless healings and providential miracles resulting in thousands of people who are now fervent followers of Christ!

**J. David Newquist, D.Min.**
*Word for Word Ministries*

§ § §

In recent years there has been a refreshing emphasis throughout the Kingdom of God regarding the relevance of spiritual fathers and mothers. The Bible is a book about the family of God, giving dozens of examples of spiritual fathers who were key in the shaping of men and women who God used to illustrate and establish the values of heaven on earth. Spiritual and emotional health are gained when we learn how to be sons and daughters in a mentoring relationship by spiritual fathers. As a result, we are empowered to personally leave a legacy of true sons and daughters who'll partner with Christ for the transformation of individuals, cities, and nations.

This book of inspiring and heart-warming stories is about ordinary people whose lives have been impacted and used by God because of the unconditional love, devoted prayer, caring admonition, demonstration of God's power, and genuine friendship of a spiritual father, Randy Conger. The transparency of the author concerning the lessons he's learned in living an authentic Christian life is affirming and challenging to both fathers, and sons and daughters in the family of God.

Whether you are young or mature in your journey of faith, I believe you will find this book of real and transparent stories to be encouraging, faith-building, and practically helpful in life, and leaving a legacy that will have lasting effects for eternity.

**Galen Gingerich**
*Lead Pastor*
*New Horizons Church*

§ § §

We spent our first in-depth conversation over lunch at Olive Garden. Randy wanted to hear about a sabbatical I had returned from about seven months before. I had been through a very difficult time in ministry a few years before and then multiple family crisis occurred in close succession leaving me on the edge of burnout. My church had been extremely gracious to send me away with full pay for a three month season of rest. It was exactly what I needed after 27 years serving at the same church. The Lord renewed my passion, my hunger for God's purposes and I fell in love with His church again.

It wasn't very long into our conversation that I realized the man sitting across the table from me was burned out. It was a bit like looking in a mirror, I could see all the signs. But Randy wasn't on the edge of burnout, he was already crispy and still smelled like smoke. As I continued to tell my story I could see in his eyes a longing for rest, but couldn't see a way out due to the current state of his small congregation. I tried to convince him how desperately he needed rest and restoration. He continued to give me reasons why he couldn't.

Even though Randy and I hadn't known each other personally, we knew of each other. There were people in my congregation who regularly attended his revival meetings at Solomon's Porch. I had heard many stories of healing and spiritual outpouring. They would also report to him about things that were happening at Life Church. He seemed pretty well informed about everything I was telling him as if spies were sending detailed accounting. It was a little creepy.

As we continued talking, the Holy Spirit began to impress upon me the importance of this man. Although he was empty and angry, he was carrying something much bigger than himself. Randy is not a snappy dresser or the kind of guy to fill the room with his personality, but a regular guy who carries weight in the Spirit. It would not be okay to walk away with a simple "I'll be praying for you." He continued to tell me how it would be impossible to take a sabbatical, so I offered for Life Church to give him a sabbatical. He was stunned. As he told me later, I called his bluff. I told him I'd have to get final approval through our stewardship team, but we would for six months pay him what his church was giving him. Life Church could be a safe haven for he and his people to be refreshed and then restart the church. Randy agreed as did our stewardship team. This began our journey together.

As Randy was renewed he decided not to restart the church, but was infused with a passion to transform the West Coast with the good news. It's a long story, but as a result, so far hundreds and hundreds of people have been led to Christ. Randy would never claim these conversions as his own as some televangelists have done, but he is comfortable in the role of a fire starter and a father. As I read his book, I was reminded of what the Holy Spirit showed me about the weight that Randy carries. The Lord has given him powerful yet practical revelation about the ability of every believer to hear the Holy Spirit and to do what Jesus did. This book and the stories told in it confirm what is possible for those who believe. As you read this book, don't view it as another history book telling stories about what great people can do. Let Randy's candor about his own fears and insecurities give you hope that if he can do it, so can you.

If you embrace the truth Randy teaches, his stories will become your stories. As you do the works of God there is no guarantee that your journey will be a walk down a rosy path. In fact, like Randy, you will be emptied out, sometimes ignored, often overlooked, but never without Christ. He will refill you, refresh you and empower you to do it again.

**Don Finley**
*Lead Pastor*
*Life Church, Salem, Oregon*

§ § §

A few years ago, the day after a late night geometry tutoring session, one of my neighbor girls knocked on my door. "I looked at colleges online today..." she said as she stepped inside.

"Wow," I said. "That's great. Good for you!"

She looked down and then looked up again with a shy smile and shining eyes. "I never believed that I could go to college before...but after yesterday, I thought maybe I could..."

That's sort of how I've felt after a late night talking and praying with Randy and crew. I've come away from a lot of them and found myself thinking, "Maybe....just maybe....I could do that too!"

Every chapter in this book contains something that has shifted the way that I live. Randy has taught me so much about the GOODNESS of God and what His heart toward me is really like. He's prayed with me for miracles in places where what we were asking for certainly seemed impossible before it happened. (And many of them did happen!) Randy taught me what forgiveness really is and what it isn't, and how to renounce lies that have separated me from the goodness of God. He has "fathered" me in what it looks like to listen to what God is saying (and takes fiendish delight in the fact that now sometimes I shake while I'm listening). He's teased me for years that he's going to take credit for every good thing I do for the rest of my life. I really hope that's actually how it works in heaven...because in a very real way, the good things that flow out of my life have Randy's fingerprints all over them.

**Christina Zeeb**
*Randy's Spiritual Daughter*

§ § §

One cool September evening I shuffled nervously up the steps into a church where I knew God was real. Stories had reached my small town of lives radically changed, of miracles coming through ordinary people, amazing whole-hearted community, and much more. I knew God was in it, it sounded just like Him.

Many stories reached my ears: my sister's life was radically changed, friends' lives were heavily impacted, and acquaintances were healed from massive injuries. I knew God was real there. I was scared. I could not stay away.

Entering the double doors those years ago, I saw free worship in all manner. Some people sat, head bowed. Some danced, some waved flags, some sang, some wrote quietly in their journals, and many prayed for others. People wandered through with coffee and brownies from down-stairs, and the children inside the entrance immediately said, "Hi." A kind man with short, fuzzy grey hair and comfortable, Birkenstock san-dals smiled, ambling over to me.

The man wasted no time, gently asking why I was there and what I wanted, and then he led me in a prayer where I gave up all my past and future, all my failures and successes to Jesus.

Randy later told me, "I could tell that you were hungry for God, hehehe." Then Randy and a couple others prophesied over me. I still remember what they said. It was good, it was healing, and I felt loved, never looked down upon.

I began attending on Friday nights regularly, watching the many pastors and workers from other churches visit to get blessed and refreshed, while I and others worshiped Jesus late into the early hours of the morning. I began finding freedom from old sins and habits, and the Bible took on amazing new life for me. This man, Randy, became a spiritual father to me in Christ, and my life continued its radical shift.

Fast-forward to the present. As a church elder, a Sunday School teacher, a small group leader, a preacher, a discipler, etc., I excitedly endorse this watershed book. I've witnessed many miracles in my own life and in the lives of others through the scriptural truth shared here.

This book will change your life forever.

Get ready.

**David Hazel**
*Randy's Spiritual Son*

# Contents

# FOREWORD

It was the summer of 1997. Donovan, my childhood church friend, was over at my parent's house one night and was talking about how he was radically changed by God. I hadn't seen him in over eight years, and I had no idea how he had lived his life. He talked about his open marriage, the drugs, alcohol, and sexual promiscuity that had eventually torn his marriage apart and brought him to his lowest threshold. His father, Tom, had just been diagnosed with terminal cancer, and yet Donovan was hopeful. His marriage shattered, perhaps beyond repair, his father dying, and yet he was hopeful.

My parents, Donovan's parents, Donovan, and I talked about our lack of passion and our desire to know God more. We decided to start meeting on Tuesday evenings. Donovan talked about this guy, Randy, who had done all of these great things for God. I was mesmerized by the stories and formed this picture of how this great man of God would be. Donovan encouraged me to ask Randy for prayer when we met on Tuesday.

1

Tuesday came. Enter Randy.

I would be lying if I didn't say I was somewhat disappointed initially. Randy wasn't flamboyant, dressed in a suit, or walking confident and tall. He was just a man. This was the Great Man of God?!?

The stories didn't match the man. You would think I would have remembered the scripture, *"But the Lord said to Samuel, 'Do not look at his appearance or at his physical stature, because I have refused him. For the Lord does not see as man sees; for man looks at the outward appearance, but the Lord looks at the heart'" (1 Samuel 6:7, NKJV).* But I didn't. I just remained puzzled by what I was told and what I saw.

We had an incredible time of confession, repentance, and revival of our hearts that evening. At the end, I asked Randy to pray for me.

You have to understand, I grew up in a very conservative church. We sang hymns and followed the same order of service every week. We did not dance or drink alcohol, and manifestations of the Holy Spirit were rare. The only one I remember is an old retired pastor jumping up one Sunday morning and running around the sanctuary yelling, "Praise the Lord." And that was radical for our church.

Randy asked me to turn my hands palms up. Kathy, Donovan's mother and long time friend, stood slightly to the side of me. I don't remember what he prayed to be honest. I flew backwards, hit my head on a table, and was completely and utterly overwhelmed by the love of God. God was real.

I had never been slain in the Spirit. I didn't even know the term. All I knew was that God was real. He touched me! I remember saying through tears, "I always knew You were real."

That night changed my walk with the Lord forever. From that night on, I had this insatiable desire to read the Bible. I consumed it. I couldn't help but pray for at least four hours a day. My greatest longing was to get on my back porch and talk with God and have Him touch me. I started having visions. Many I didn't understand. I began to dream dreams. I had these spiritual warnings and information about others that made me feel a little crazy. I called Tom. (I didn't even know how to contact Randy.) Tom arranged a meeting over coffee with Randy. That was the beginning of my journey with my spiritual father.

Reading through this book was like taking a step into my past and remembering the great exploits of God. I couldn't help but find myself remembering my own stories of miracles that God had done. I felt this momentum growing in my own spirit. This cry that says, "I want to live like that. Do it again, God!" The strength and inspiration that these stories and instructions provide must be similar to what David did when he "strengthened himself in the Lord" (1 Samuel 30:6). It is no wonder that the Jews throughout the Old Testament made altars to remember what God had done in various places. These places were their faith builders, their strength to go on, and their reminder that God was alive and active in their lives. Once you live a life – where you see the miracles of God continually, you are wrecked. You can't go back to mundane everyday life you know there is more. And it never gets old.

I feel so privileged to have grown up in my spiritual life with such an amazing spiritual father. To know Randy is to know God's love. Never have I known someone so sacrificial, who can continue to love and demonstrate grace when others would walk away. I try not to compare, but his example is compelling. He is the only person I know to whom I can bring the most shameful, hurtful places of my life and receive non-judgmental counsel. He will confront me, even when it hurts (I honestly believe his confrontations with me over the years have pained him more than me). In the deepest and darkest nights of my own soul, Randy would be present seeking to understand the depths of my pain and encouraging me to hear from God. I have been the beneficiary of learning how to go to God and hear from Him even when my pain is overwhelming and I have no understanding. I can still declare the goodness of God in these places of my life, which is a miracle if you knew me 17 years ago.

Just recently, I watched my 22 year old daughter go through her own dark, painful night of her soul. Her response was utterly amazing. She went to the beach, because she knew she and God needed to have a conversation. She recognized that the wall between her and God was of her own making. She consciously let down her wall and she was able to hear God speak to her, and she worshiped Him despite her circumstances. How amazing that she knows how to hear God's voice, let alone hear His voice when she is hurting. This is what spiritual fathers teach. This is Randy's legacy.

**Annie Korkeakoski-Sears**
*Assistant Pastor*
*Solomon's Porch Ministries*

# THE BEGINNING

## My education begins

The restaurant bustled with the lunch time crowd. Across from me sat a small, timid, not quite middle-aged lady. Her demeanor emphasized her small stature. She trembled constantly and spoke in a whisper barely discernible over the crowd noise. Sitting in an almost fetal position, she would not look me in the eyes.

A week before, I had led her in the sinners' prayer, the result of an amazing divine appointment and encounter with God. She had been suicidal, but now for the first time she had some hope, though only a little. I had tried to get her to go to church with me or even a home meeting, but to no avail. She was too afraid. I had prayed and prayed for her. She needed Him desperately. It was obvious that there was some real spiritual warfare going on.

Trying to help her, I set up times for a mini Bible Study, designed just for her. This was our third such meeting. The scripture I chose was:

> For we wrestle not against flesh and blood, but against principali-
> ties, against powers, against the rulers of the darkness of this world,
> against spiritual wickedness in high places (Ephesians 6:12, KJV).

I began by telling her that just as there was a God who was a heavenly father who loved her, there was also an enemy who hated her. I looked down and read the scripture out loud to her. When I looked back up, I received one of the biggest shocks of my life.

The person sitting across from me was no longer a small, timid creature but a bold, arrogant, and threatening one. I swear that even her facial features had changed! She leaned across the table toward me with eyes of pure hatred and said in a man's voice, "So, what are you going to do about it?"

Now, a little information about myself at that point in my life. Close to 30 years old, I was married with two children. I was a small business owner and a zealous Christian, passionate about leading people to Christ. I had already witnessed many healing miracles, and I was aware of the supernatural.

But nothing like this. My education was about to begin.

Back to the restaurant. I immediately tried to conquer the fear rising inside me and act like a real Christian with authority. There was no point in trying to talk to my friend, so I answered the demon as boldly as I could, "In the name of Jesus, you have to leave."

What happened next shook my faith.

The demon actually calmed a bit, looked at me and said, "It didn't work. I'm still here." The fight was on. Why didn't it work? This wasn't how things were supposed to go! The demons were supposed to obey my commands in Jesus' name.

Over and over I commanded. I pled the blood of Jesus, I did everything I had heard or read to do. Nothing worked and all the while the demon was taunting me.

Finally he screeched in a very loud voice, so that everyone in the restaurant could hear, "What's the matter? Has your God left you? Ha, ha, ha! Your God has left you!"

All these years later I can still hear that voice and feel the shame and bewilderment that I felt when I simply got up and left, leaving my new friend to deal with her demon alone.

Of course, the story doesn't end there. You may wonder why this story is in the book in the first place. People don't normally advertise their failures in a Christian book, especially not one where the enemy wins the battle.

But this is exactly why I wrote this book.

The vast difference between the theories that I believed from Bible stories etc. and my own experience confronted me. I don't mean that anything in the Bible is just theoretical. It is just that without experience, our understanding is always incomplete.

If only I could have had someone who had already been through a battle like this to direct and help me! Oh how things would have been different! Sadly, I had to figure it out mostly by myself. I say "by myself," but that is excluding the one Person who made all the difference, the Holy Spirit.

Back to the story...

A couple hours later my friend called me on the phone (she was herself again). "Where did you go?" she asked.

"Don't you remember what happened?" I replied. She had no memory of the confrontation and was now even more afraid and desperate than ever.

Not wanting a repeat performance of the scene from the restaurant, I told her that I could not help her alone and that we would have to go to my friend's house for prayer. She pleaded for another way, but I knew that I needed help with this one. Finally, she agreed to go with me to the house of a friend of mine.

The half hour drive into Salem with just the two of us in the car lasted for ages. The demon manifested the whole way, carrying on a conversation full of threats and boasts of his power. He boasted about the futility of my attempts to get rid of him and his friends, all of whom claimed ownership of this woman.

That night was a nightmare. I had never encountered a struggle like that before. I learned that my friend had been a witch. She was raised as a child in a witch's coven, where her father was still the reigning warlock. As we prayed for her (with many others in a back room praying for us), the threats and cursing intensified. At one point the demon threatened to kill her if we didn't stop. When we tried to restrain her from hurting herself, she literally threw us across the room. Both of us were over 200 lbs.

The fear inside of me grew so bad that it was actually hard to breathe. I had to leave the house and go for a walk to pray. With renewed faith, I returned. After another hour long spiritual power struggle, the demon left.

Wow, I was glad it was over! But it wasn't. The next day I got a call from her husband wondering what was going on and why his wife was acting so strangely.

I won't bore you with all the events over the following weeks, but they included phone call after phone call, meetings, prayer and power encounters, casting demons out that only came back the next day, suicide attempts that I felt responsible for, and mental health professionals who offered nothing more than drugs and confinement. I was exhausted and even suffering from spiritual warfare of my own in the form of a painful abscessed tooth that wouldn't heal.

One day I knew we were finally getting close. We had identified a number of reasons (open doors) that allowed the demons to come back, and we were no longer dealing with the one who had confronted me in the restaurant but instead one of his superiors. We were tired, tired of all of this and even wondering if the enemy sent this whole ordeal to distract us from other ministry opportunities. At one really intense point during prayer, she jumped up and ran out of the room. We just let her go, taking the opportunity to rest.

Finally, I got up and went to look for her. She had to be in the building somewhere. I found her huddled on the floor in a back hallway, clutching a very large butcher knife that she must have found in the church kitchen.

Upon seeing me, she rose and walked toward me; only it wasn't her, it was the demon. With eyes of hate and in the same menacing male voice I had grown used to, the demon threatened, "I am going to kill you!" as he aimed the knife at me.

At that moment I heard the still small voice of the Holy Spirit inside of me saying, "Stand your ground." The arguments inside of my head were screaming, "I am going to die!" and "You know how well commanding it to stop in Jesus' name has worked so far!" Fearfully, I didn't know what to do, but I stood still.

She walked toward me until the knife pressed against my chest. The demon kept threatening me, "I am going to kill you!" I honestly wondered why it hadn't already. Then I heard that still small voice again: "She won't let him." Something clicked inside of me. "No!" I said. "You won't kill me, because Mary (not her real name) won't let you! She loves me." He threatened again, and I responded again: "She won't let you. She loves me!"

At this point, Mary fell to the floor in a heap. The knife fell away, the demon left, and she was free! I wish I could say that the story ends here, but it doesn't; however, what we learned eventually led to her complete healing.

Like a heroin addict needs to learn to live without the drugs even after the drugs have left the body, Mary had to learn her authority in Jesus to keep the enemy away. It took a little while, but she did.

To this day, some thirty years later my friend Mary is still free.

Nothing in my reading or past experience had prepared me for this ordeal. I would gladly have sought help if I had known anybody that I trusted who had experience and knew what to do. Sadly, most of the pastors I knew at the time either didn't even believe that demons existed anymore, or they would tell me to simply command the demon to go in the name of Jesus.

Surely there is a better way than everyone learning these kinds of lessons by themselves! It is my hope that others who come after me can learn from the stories of my experiences. Every circumstance is different.

I certainly cannot take away all the risks that come with your learning. But if I can save someone else even a little bit of the heartache and trouble that I experienced, then telling my stories will be worth it.

I am now much older. My wife and I have four children and four grand-children. I have held many roles in the body of Christ, but by far the one I value the most is that of a spiritual father. I measure the success of my ministry not by the size of the building or the number in my congregation, but by the success of those that I consider my "spiritual kids."

## *Helping people learn what they think they already know…*

Just like with natural children, real life lessons are rarely learned through one conversation. In real life it really is, "here a little, there a little." This is especially true when teaching about the mystical things of God like gifts of the Spirit or healing. Wouldn't it be great if a mother only had to tell her children one time to clean their rooms or wash their hands, and for the rest of their lives kids did just that? It's just not going to happen. In the same way, it would be totally unreasonable for me to expect that if I preach one sermon or have one conversation, my "kids" would get it and live out that truth for the rest of their lives.

Reality and theory are often two very different things. Before I actually learned to drive, I thought: "You turn the key, you turn the wheel, and push the pedals. What's the big deal?" Contrary to what I believed, I needed someone to teach me. Having good information from reading the driver's manual or the owner's manual for my car would not have been enough to help me become a good driver. In driving, and in life, most (if not all) of us need a patient coach. We learn and grow when someone cares enough for us to put their own life on the line to teach us what they have already learned, not from books but from experience.

This is why Jesus had disciples, not just students. He didn't just teach a class. He modeled for them how to do something, taught them about it, and then had them do it. He instructed and corrected them as they went along, knowing full well that someday they were going to have to do it on their own and that someday they would become teachers themselves.

One of the obstacles Jesus had in teaching His followers is that they already had so many misconceptions about the subject matter that He taught. He often had to prove to them the difference between what they currently thought and what He was trying to teach.

All too often, I have the same experience. I am teaching or counseling and my spiritual son or daughter truly believes that they already understand what I am trying to teach them. This is really frustrating for both of us. The student is tired of hearing the same old things from me, and I am tired of trying to find new ways of communicating the same concepts. I hit that point once with Joey, one of my spiritual sons, and it escalated into an argument in a local restaurant.

"Randy, I get it," Joey snapped. "You have told me over and over! I get it!"

"I know that you think you understand me and you can repeat back to me everything that I am saying," I explained, "but you still don't get it." As I was trying to illustrate my point, I noticed a ketchup bottle sitting on the table. I picked it up and said, "It is as if I am telling you that this bottle is red and you say, 'I know it is red!' But "red" means something different to you than it does to me."

We left in frustration. Sometime later, Joey received a huge revelation that changed his life. He couldn't wait to tell me about it! (It was the same thing I had been trying and trying to explain to him in the restaurant.)

"Joey," I said, "THAT is what I was trying to tell you!"

"I know that NOW..." he laughed. "It IS red!"

This vague, senseless saying has become code for us ever since. Whenever one of us is trying to communicate something that we are sure the other just does not understand we just say, "It is red!"

When I am trying to explain something that is "red," usually I will tell a story to explain what I mean. I use my own life experiences as a testimony to the faithfulness of God and as a tool to try to teach what are sometimes mysteries to people today. I try my best to do what the apostles did:

> *"As for us, we cannot help speaking about what we have seen and heard" (Acts 4:20, NIV); or again, "That which was from the beginning, which we have heard, which we have seen with our eyes, which we have looked at and our hands have touched, this we proclaim concerning the Word of life" (1 John 1:1, NIV).*

## *Let My Ceiling Be Your Floor*

Sometimes I repeat myself... a lot. My spiritual family teases me relentlessly for sharing the same stories over and over again. So what if I repeat them? I wouldn't have to repeat them if they would just get it the first time, right? No wonder I like speaking overseas or in other churches where they haven't already heard my stories!

One night I drove home from a very late meeting thinking about something that I was still having trouble communicating to the group, something they still didn't quite understand, which I thought would help them so much in their walk with the Lord. While I prayed about this, I thought I heard the Lord say: "Leave them a book of your stories so that not only will they get it, but so will their children." You might say that this book is my legacy to them, and to you.

If you are reading this and you are not someone who I have had the honor to "father" in person, please let me give you an insight into the intentions of my heart. This book is not intended to be an autobiography. It is intended to be a teaching tool. The reason that I tell stories of things that I have done in my life with God is that I genuinely believe that if I can do it, you can do it even better!

I have been so blessed by God to have had a life of many adventures in serving Him. I literally have thousands of stories, each one precious to me, and only some that I can share. Every one of my stories is an invitation to you, that anything is possible for you. At Bethel Church in Redding, California they have a saying that goes something like: "My ceiling can become your floor." The intent is that as I push into the things of God, I can create doors for others to enter more easily. I hope my ceiling becomes your floor. I try to live to be an example. Sometimes my mistakes or failures are my best teaching tools for others today. If somehow I can save you from having to learn the hard way, then my mistakes have value.

I am SO very proud of the men and women who have let me disciple and teach them. I expect every one of them to exceed me in every way. I tease them by telling them, "I am going to take credit for everything you ever do." Some of them are pastors in their own right, and I half expect them to take exception to a statement like that. After all, I'm not the only person who has poured into their lives over the years. But so far, each one of them has taken my pride in them as a compliment and been thankful that I think so highly of them, that I believe they are capable of great exploits with God. And I do!

The Lord told me once that my spiritual kids would be exceptional anywhere in the world. I agree.

# WHAT IS A SPIRITUAL FATHER

*For though you might have ten thousand instructors in Christ, yet you do not have many fathers...*

If I were a conspiracy theorist, I would believe that there is a conspiracy to belittle, demean and destroy the image of fathers. The father image proposed by the media, especially TV, is that of an arrogant, bumbling idiot who cares for no one but himself. Children's programming is the worst! Children are portrayed as wise and capable, while fathers are portrayed as ignorant and helpless. Almost as if by some evil design, each generation must figure things out for themselves.

This wedge between parents and children creates generation after generation of people who might as well be orphans! As a pastor, I have met very few people who do not claim to come from a dysfunctional family. It is incredibly sad.

### *Honor Your Father and Mother*

One of the first things I do to disciple people is to teach them to appreciate their parents:

> *"Honor your father and mother (which is the first commandment with a promise), so that it may be well with you, and that you may live long on the earth" (Ephesians 6:2–3, NASB).*

I teach them that God has an inheritance intended for them that is released through honor. If we honor our parents, we can receive our inheritance, even if it is made up of good things that our parents never received or experienced for themselves. Honoring our parents does not mean to obey their every command; it means to thank God for them. Instead of judging all their faults, thank God for your parents and search out the blessings that God intended for you to inherit for free!

### *Spiritual Fathers and Mothers*

Fathers are not perfect people. They never have been. There are no perfect people. Fathers are people who choose to have children. I don't just mean that they choose to have sex and procreate. I mean that they choose to become fathers. Usually, just as with natural fathers, "we don't choose our spiritual fathers, they choose us."

If you are blessed to have someone like this in your life, you will already understand what I mean. Spiritual fathers are not necessarily people who know everything, teach classes, or preach. We can learn a lot from teachers and preachers, but that is not the same as having a spiritual father.

A spiritual father or mother is someone who has taken a personal interest in YOU. They have attached their own destiny to yours. They see their own success in seeing you succeed. They believe in you long before you believe in yourself. They care enough about you to pray for you, to seek the Lord on your behalf, to intercede when you are wrong, and to cheer when you overcome each obstacle that you face. They may not be the best, richest, or most famous person you know. However, as a spiritual parent, whatever they do have, they are more than willing to pass on to you!

I have had some great teachers in my life. Some I met personally, like John Wimber and Demos Shakarian. These men truly changed my life through their examples and teaching, but they were not spiritual fathers to me in the sense I am describing here. Time and distance didn't allow them to really know me. I could not share my failures, my fears, or doubts with these men.

## Graham, One of My Spiritual Fathers

My spiritual fathers have been men like Graham Phillips, who was pastor of My Father's Vineyard in Salem, Oregon. Graham wasn't perfect, but he believed in me. He believed in me even before I did! He invested his time and his heart in me. When I had doubts or struggles, I didn't have to hide my inadequacies from him. He coached me and challenged me with more than I thought I could ever do. Graham told me that I had value, worth, a calling, and a God given destiny. When Graham spoke into my life, he demonstrated his words with action. He gave me his pulpit. He risked his own reputation when he called upon the church to recognize the pastoral gift that was on me.

By supporting me in the way he did, Graham opened doors for me, doors that I may never have earned the favor or respect to gain access to myself. Other pastors and leaders treated me with a respect I had not yet earned, because Graham believed in me.

I will never forget walking away from a desperate hospital visit, struggling with the weight of grief from the family's seemingly hopeless circumstances. "So, this is the ministry?" I asked. "Yes," Graham replied. "This is the ministry." Coming alongside people in their time of crisis was actually far more important than how well I could speak from the pulpit. Helping them hear and see God when tears and demonic accusations assaulted them was my assignment.

Along the way I discovered the most important thing I learned about ministry: I didn't have to be perfect or even good enough. God was always faithful. He seemed genuinely pleased to have me as his representative as we ministered together. A friend of mine said it this way, "God can still draw a straight line with a crooked stick." In God's hands, I could do and be far more than I ever dreamed or imagined. Graham saw this long before I did.

## Pioneer

One day Graham came to my house. After dropping off his wife, Gladys, and daughter, Esther, to fellowship with my wife and kids, he said, "Let's go for a ride." As we were driving in his car, he put on a cassette with a very old song.

"Randy," he said, "this song is talking about you."

The song was Pioneer, by Honey Tree: (the lyrics can be found online at: http://www.songlyrics.com/rick-pino/pioneer-lyrics/), these lyrics truly described my heart and the sometimes lonely road of pressing into the deeper things of God so that "others who follow after you can use the road."

Since that time, my accomplishments have always been for the benefit of those who would come after me. The words of this song have been like a prophetic word from God that He has used to encourage and comfort me again and again.

Spiritual fathers are intentional trail blazers, pioneers making a way so that their kids can accomplish the same feat in less time and with less effort than they did. Their goal is for their children to exceed them in every way.

## *A Father's Pride*

One night I accepted a "friend request" on Facebook from someone I had not seen for many years. I think the last time I had seen her was soon after a stay in a drug rehab facility after another relapse with meth. At that time, she had a son that she was trying desperately to keep. As we chatted she told me that she was now married, had four children, loved the Lord, and was thankful for all I had taught her all those years ago.

I told her that I was proud of her. Really, who was I to say that I was proud of her? She has had many teachers other than me; she had learned so much more than I had ever taught her. True, I had believed in her when others didn't. I loved her and invested in her but so had others, some more than me. She told me that it meant a lot to her to hear those words from me. Which, of course, is why I said it!

How I would love to be able to hear my dad (or Graham, they have both gone on to glory) say he was proud of me. My heavenly Father does it often and that is better than anything, but we all have that little longing in our heart for Dad's approval.

19

### *Adoption*

Joey is one of my spiritual sons. When I first met Joey, he was a teen-ager who already loved the Lord. He was zealous for the things of God and evangelism. Signs, wonders, and demonstrations of God's presence were his goals. He longed for them. I did not teach him these things; he already had them.

Growing up, Joey had been hurt in church and misunderstood by lead-ers. He had harshly judged his parents. In the process, he judged himself without even realizing what he was doing. My role in Joey's life was much more than a pastor speaking from a pulpit or classroom. Before he even knew what was happening, I had adopted him.

Don't get me wrong, I did NOT want to replace his earthly father. In fact, my very first goal was to repair that relationship! Nor did I want to teach him that I was a good church leader and the others were bad. I wanted to repair those relationships as well.

All of these things (and many more life lessons like those in this book) take time, lots of time. It requires relationship. Now mind you, no matter how much I wanted to teach Joey, it would not have mattered if he didn't want to be a "son." To his great credit, through all of the trials, ups and downs of ministry and life, Joey still calls me dad, to which I respond, "All that I have is yours."

When Joey went with me to Africa, I had already been there. By God's grace I had gained favor with many people, and they came expecting great things from God. One night when everyone expected me to teach, I introduced Joey instead. I did so in a very embarrassing fashion, getting everyone to chant, "Joey, Joey…"

By the time Joey stood, he did not need to start from scratch and impress everyone with his gifts before they would receive him. No, he stood on the ground already plowed with my reputation and recognition. When he spoke it was like a representation of me, only better. I don't even know how many were saved, delivered, and healed that night, but it was one of the best nights I have ever experienced. Was I jealous? No! I WAS PROUD.

## *A Definition*

In this book I intentionally use the word "father" instead of "mentor" because the level of intimacy as a spiritual parent is so much deeper than that of a mentor. As a spiritual father, I have both sons and daughters. Spiritual mothers have sons and daughters as well.

A spiritual father/son relationship is not what some would expect. It is a relationship in every sense of the word. You don't have to be older to be a father, and you don't have to submit to be a son. Some people might picture spiritual fathering as an old sage dishing out wise words to young plebes eating them all up. They would be wrong.

The capacity to be a spiritual father or mother has nothing to do with age and everything to do with intentional investment. All you have to do is care, care enough to share anything you might have that could possibly benefit someone you care about.

To be a son or daughter, you simply need to appreciate and value the gifts you're being given. You don't have to do everything like the fathers or mothers who are investing in you, but you do need to give a little extra weight to the information given to you by someone who has demonstrated that they are truly looking out for your best interest.

In 2013 I witnessed an extraordinary son who recognized the value of having fathers in his life. To be honest, he made me jealous.

His name is Tony Kim, and he is the pastor of Renaissance Church in Bakersfield, California. His church probably had seating for 100 people, and yet here he was putting on a conference with three world renowned speakers. I could only think of what it would mean to my church to have even one of these speakers come. Yet here they were: Che Ahn, James Goll and Wesley Campbell, all speaking at one place over the weekend. How could he do it?

Che Ahn explained it one night as he stood up to receive an offering, not for himself or the honorariums for these speakers, but for Renaissance Church. You see, Tony was his spiritual son. Che Ahn was not here to advance his own ministry, but Tony's. He wanted to see Tony succeed. The other speakers also came to invest in what God was doing at Renaissance Church.

I was so impressed that I went back some months later and met with Tony to find out what made him so special. What I found out was that while Tony is a great guy with wonderful gifting and passion for the Lord, his real gift is in knowing how to be a son. He has learned to value the gifts of fathers.

Jesus told us to *"Go and make disciples..." (Matthew 28:19).* I don't think He meant for that to be some class where students learn to repeat all the correct doctrines. I think He meant for us to go and pour into others what we have. Even if we have very little and have just been saved, we can care enough to pour out what we have and invest in someone else.

In this book, I have tried to leave a legacy, an inheritance if you will, to those who are willing to receive it. If you were my spiritual kid, these are things I would share with you. I wish I could hug every one of you, look you in the eye, and tell you how valuable you are! You are worthy of having someone who wants to hear your dreams and visions, someone who wants to take the time to partner with you to see those things come to pass. That is truly what your heavenly Father is like. As I write, I am praying that your heavenly Father will speak to you through the words I've written and send fathers and mothers, who will love you and believe in you like He does, to walk alongside you in your journey.

# WHAT IS GOD SAYING

*You can know for yourself*

Whenever I meet with someone, (you know, one of those "we need to meet with the pastor" type of meetings), I usually spend a good deal of time drinking coffee and listening as they try to impress upon me how dire their situation is. Whatever the problem, my response always is: "What is God saying to you about this?" I say it so often that one person I counseled told me that when I die my headstone will read, "What is God saying now?"

I am a very empathic person, and it's not that I don't care about the problem. It's just that whenever we are in crisis we seem overly aware of what the enemy (satan) is saying, and due to our fear or frustration we often don't have a clue what God is saying! When I ask, "What is God saying to you about this?" the answer to the question is almost always, "I don't know."

"Well," I tell them, "I guess finding out should be our first objective then, shouldn't it?"

Ah, but here is the problem. We, as Christians, who claim to have been saved into a relationship with Jesus, have often relegated ourselves to a relationship through a rule book alone. Many Christians don't even know much of what the book says! We struggle to live FOR the God who said He would never leave us or forsake us, but we do this without His direct input. We call Him Lord (boss), but have no means of receiving applicable instructions from Him about our current situation. We lose track of His very nature, which is to help. We don't realize that He wants to walk with us through all of life's trials.

As you're reading this, objections may come to mind.

You might say, "Hearing from God is so subjective."

Or, "What about the postal worker who killed all those people and said that God told him to?"

Or, "I tried that once and made a big fool of myself."

It is true that people who are trying to hear from God sometimes make mistakes. Frankly, I have heard some really crazy things from people who claim to hear from God, some of which I'm sure He didn't actually say. So much so that it almost causes me to repent of my own teaching and tell people to just stick to the Word (Bible), because it would seem safer than teaching them to listen to God's voice.

Sticking to the Word is always good counsel. God will NEVER say anything that contradicts what He has already said in Scripture. But then again, I hear some pretty wild claims from people who "stick to the Word" and then interpret Scripture to say what they want it to say.

Slavery, wife beating, and all sorts of things that are contrary to the nature of God have been justified as God's will by people who claim to stick to the Word.

## Learn to Pray God's Heart

As an example of misusing Scripture, one man told me that he prayed according to the Scripture, *"If you ask me anything in my name, I will do it" (John 14:14, NKJV).* So he prayed that God would MAKE his wife come back to him. He couldn't understand why God had not answered his prayer, given that the Bible said to pray this way.

I explained that God does not MAKE anyone do anything. He gave her a free will and though it may be God's will that they be together, God would not overrule her will, even if my friend prayed and asked Him to do it in Jesus' name. I told him that it would be better to pray and ask the Lord how to pray FOR his wife, how to intercede for her and her needs, asking the Lord what He was doing in her life.

I continue to teach and instruct people on how they can hear from God for themselves. If we ask Him, "Father, what are you doing?" rather than try to manipulate another person's will with our prayers, we can pray according to God's will by asking Him to do what He is doing in the situation.

## Trust Me

Recently, I met with a very depressed Christian woman. She was going through a divorce, praying that God would restore her marriage. The day before, her husband had suggested selling their wedding rings to pay bills, which left her devastated. As I met with her for the very first time, I asked my question, "What is God saying to you about this?"

She replied that she didn't hear from God and that she didn't know how.

To be honest, I felt so sorry for her that I was surprised by what I "heard" the still, small voice within me say in response. Shocking her, her friend, and even myself, I replied, "I am sorry, I don't believe you."

She looked at me, hurt and insulted. She probably wondered how I could be so cruel at a time like this. So I explained, *"Jesus said, 'I am the Good Shepherd and my sheep hear my voice'"(John 10:14, 27, my paraphrase).* You are obviously a Christian, one of His sheep, and He says that you DO hear Him. I am sorry, but I have to choose to believe Him instead of you."

To my relief, she softened and said, "All I hear Him say is, 'Trust Me.'"

I sighed. "Yes, that sounds just like Him."

God seldom speaks to me the way I would like Him to. He rarely explains things in detail, but two words from Him can say volumes.

"Trust Me," from God means, "Everything is going to be all right. No matter what happens, I will take care of you." "Trust Me" means that He is with me. I don't have to try to figure everything out alone. It means that He is on the job, and I don't need to worry.

A couple of nights later, the same lady came to one of our meetings. We had a guest speaker that night, a man very gifted in the word of knowledge and prophecy. During his message, he called her out and said, "Lady, I don't know you, but I sense from the Lord that you are going through a very tough time and that God is saying to you to just trust Him." Wow, what a confirmation!

I don't know what has happened regarding her marriage, but I do know that she is now secure in the fact that God is with her and whatever happens she will be okay. She came away knowing God's reality and presence with her in a personal way.

## Doing What the Father Is Doing

When we learn to listen to God's voice, He not only comforts our hearts and leads us personally, but He also leads us into doing the work of the Kingdom. Miracles of all shapes and sizes naturally follow when we listen to God's still, small voice and obey Him.

I have lots of stories like this. Many are stories about miracles and healing that resulted from following the leading of the Holy Spirit through that still, small voice. I like to tell people that if God said, "Say 'Open'," even I could split the Red Sea like Moses! And it is true, I have seen more healings and people come to the Lord than I could count. I have seen blind eyes and deaf ears opened. I have seen the lame walk. Did those things happen because I am so gifted? Nah, I don't think so. I don't mean to belittle the gifts that God has given me, but I really believe these results are available to any believer willing to listen and obey the voice of the Holy Spirit.

Even though I have been ministering to people for forty years, I have little confidence in my own knowledge or experience. With every encounter I pray "Lord they need You, not me."

Jesus said that He could do nothing by Himself. If He couldn't, I certainly can't! Jesus said He only did what He saw the Father doing: *"I tell you the truth, the Son can do nothing by himself. He does only what he sees the Father doing" (John 5:19, NLT)*. And He also said, *"As the Father has sent me, so I am sending you" (John 20:21, NLT)*. Time and again, I have seen miracles just by the leading of that still, small voice.

Sometimes God's still, small voice leads us to do things we would never do on our own.

## *Deaf Ears Healed*

When Joey went with me on the mission trip to Uganda as he ministered to people during the altar call, a woman asked for prayer for her deaf ear. Joey did his best, claiming Scripture and praying for all he was worth, but nothing happened. Then he thought he saw a picture from the Lord of himself spitting on his finger and putting it in her ear. Joey's first response was, "Lord, I can't do that. It's gross!" But finally he told the woman what he saw and asked if it would be okay. She said to go ahead, and so he did. He put his finger in his mouth, swished it around, put it in her ear and commanded the ear to open. Afterward he asked if anything had happened, and she replied that she was healed. He decided to test the healing by having her cover her good ear as he progressively stepped back, asking, "Can you hear me now?" Eventually, halfway across the room it hit him, she really was healed! Man of faith and power that he was, his response was an excited, "NO WAY!!"

Later that year, I had Joey share this testimony at a men's retreat here in the United States. One pastor asked if the woman was healed because we were in Africa and miracles just happen more frequently there. I responded, "I used to believe that, but I don't anymore. I've learned that no matter where you go, there you are, and if you don't believe in healing here, you won't believe in healing there either."

At this retreat, an old man, also deaf in one ear, came forward for prayer. Joey asked the Lord how he should pray and heard to do the same thing. This man was also completely healed, even though he had undergone many surgeries to no avail.

God simply looks for people who will hear His voice and obey.

Most of the time being led by the Spirit is like dancing with God. He is right there with you. It's a beautiful and exciting experience. But if you're going to dance with God, you should know: He likes to lead.

## Blind Man Healed

Before we went to Africa, Joey's sister had a dream about the trip. In the dream, she saw a tall black man who was blind in one eye and had something wrong with his left knee. The dream was so vivid that when she woke up, she drew a picture of the man and gave it to Joey. Sure enough, while speaking in a village church, a man stood up for prayer. Even before he told us what was wrong with him, we knew that he was the man in the drawing. Joey excitedly shook my arm, showing me the drawing saying, "It's him, Randy. It's HIM!" The man was blind in one eye (his whole eyeball was covered in white) and lame in his left knee.

How hard do you think it was to pray in faith for this man's healing? God had told us about him and sent us to the other side of the world to meet him. We were confident that God was going to heal him, so confident that we weren't even fazed when after we prayed he could only see shadows. We prayed again and again, until at last we watched as the white film covering his eye completely disappeared and he could see perfectly. Was this man healed because we had so much faith or were so gifted? No, we had just heard from God.

## How Do We Know It's Him?

If we believe God's Word is true and that He is speaking to us today, how can we tell if and when He is speaking? In short, the best way to know whether or not He is speaking is to know him. The apostle Paul is a great role model here. He told us that he considered all of his training and accomplishments as mere rubbish compared to knowing Jesus *(See Philippians 3:8)*.

To illustrate this point I ask people, "If someone came up to you and told you that I said I hate you, would you believe them?" The answer is, "No, of course not." Why? Because anyone who knows me knows that I would never say that about anyone. It's as simple as that. In the same way, if you hear a voice telling you that God is disgusted with you (as if He is at the end of His patience with you), you can know that it is not from Him because He has said that He loves you and that He would never leave you *(See Hebrews 13:5b)*.

Hearing from God comes as a result of relationship. When I first got saved, I didn't know the Bible very well and didn't know Him very well. As a result, I couldn't hear very well. I thought that other people must be more special than me. I wondered if they had a phone line in their head directly to God because it seemed that they always heard from Him and I didn't.

The more I tried, the more frustrated I got. I began to hear more voices, but I couldn't tell which, if any of them, was God. I thought I was going crazy. I did not realize that I expected intimate conversation with someone who I had never been intimate with. I was rejecting what God was actually saying because I was expecting him to say something different or to say it in a different way. Even today that can happen to me. Learning to listen to God has been a process that grows out of a deepening relationship with Him. It has taken time and practice.

### *Learning to Listen*

What about you? Are you ready to practice listening to what God is saying to you today?

First let me describe some of the ways that God speaks to us. The most common is the "still, small voice" (*1 Kings 19*). God can also speak through what I call "the witness of the Spirit" (*1 John 5*). Additionally, dreams, visions, and even an audible voice can reveal a message from God. For me, it is often a combination of ways that He speaks. For instance, I will receive a "witness in my spirit" while reading a scripture. It seems as if the Holy Spirit is simply saying, "Pay attention to this!" Then, the scripture becomes the actual message. The same thing could happen with a vision or mental image.

## *The Witness of the Spirit*

Not all dreams, visions, or voices are from God, but the simple witness of the Spirit is my best tool to recognize when God is speaking to me.

For me, the description of the Urim and Thummim in the priest's breastplate best describes how this works. In the book of Exodus we have this verse:

> *And you shall put in the breastplate of judgment the Urim and the Thummim, and they shall be over Aaron's heart when he goes in before the Lord. So Aaron shall bear the judgment of the children of Israel over his heart before the Lord continually (Exodus 28:30, NKJV).*

The Urim and Thummim were stones put in the breastplate of the high priest. With these stones, the priest could discern a simple "Yes" or "No" answer from the Lord about any decision he needed to make. Some say that either one would glow or the other. Please understand, these were not magical stones. They were simply a way that God had chosen to speak.

Yes or No? That doesn't seem like much information until you consider that all computers today are built on the simple "X or O" concept. Even the most complex graphics are built with this simple "Yes or No."

I believe that God has put this ability within every believer, as we all have the Holy Spirit within us. He calls us kings and priests *(Revelation 1:6)*.

Should we all go out and buy magical stones in order to hear God? Of course not! There is no such thing. But we can all learn to sense the simple witness inside of us. This witness of the Spirit could best be described as a "sense" or feeling in our own spirit.

## *The Mechanics of "Hearing"*

We know that as humans we are made up of three parts. First, we are spiritual beings; this is the part of us that is "made alive" when we are born again. Second, we have a soul, which is most commonly defined as our mind, will, and emotions. Third, we live in a body. English words and Western culture do not define these parts very well, but this example may help:

> If I touch a hot stove, I will feel the heat (body).
>
> If someone says something mean to me, I may get my feelings hurt (soul).
>
> If I walk into a room where an argument has just occurred, I may feel that something is not right (spirit).
>
> We can do the same thing with the word "hear:"
>
> I hear sound with my ears (body).
>
> I hear thoughts in my brain (soul).
>
> I hear God speak to my heart (spirit).

In the book of John (3:1–8), we have Jesus explaining this spiritual reality to a religious man, Nicodemus, who was having a hard time understanding. When He said, "You must be born again," Nicodemus asked, "What?!? Return again to my mother's womb?" Jesus used the wind as an example of something that Nicodemus couldn't see but was aware that it existed.

Jesus also said this:

> "For God is Spirit, so those who worship him must worship in spirit and in truth" (John 4:24, NLT).

I think of it this way. God is a spirit. When God speaks, He most often speaks to MY SPIRIT. It is the job of my mind to translate. That is why my Spanish speaking friends hear Him in Spanish, and I hear Him in English. This is also why some things He actually says can be misinterpreted. My mind is limited to what I have learned or experienced from my past. If I have a view of God as an angry judge who is just looking for me to mess up, I may not hear Him say "I love you" at all. I simply won't recognize "I love you" as coming from Him.

Our language is often a huge barrier to those who think they don't "hear." We commonly use words such as heart or conscience to describe our spirit.

When I say, "Listen to your heart," I am not talking about the organ that pumps blood. I am talking about the center of your being: your spirit. This hearing could often be called a feeling. Not like hot or cold (body), or an emotion (soul), but a sense in your spirit, something you seem to know, but don't know how you know.

I use words like "confirmation" or "a check in my spirit" to describe these feelings, where it feels as if God is saying yes or no. A sense of His presence means yes. A sense of troubling or unsettledness means no. Often I will hear someone speaking, and just one word or phrase will stand out.

It will feel like those words have God's fingerprints all over them. I take this to mean God is telling me to pay attention.

## *An Experiment*

Let's try a little experiment. The best and simplest way to hear from God is through Scripture. As I said before, God will never contradict Himself. We know that Scripture is His Word. Listening as we read His Word can teach us what His voice sounds like.

Now, for our experiment, open your Bible. If you want, you can even ask God where to read; but God can speak to you about your current situation from almost anywhere in the Word. Pray, "God, please speak to me through Your Word."

Then begin by reading no more than a chapter. As you read, listen to your heart. In most cases, a verse or phrase will stick out, almost as if it is highlighted on the page. It is for you. Whether this happens or not, meditate on what you read throughout the day, "listening to your heart." I am confident that something you read will become personal to you.

> *Hebrews 11:6 (NLT) says, "Anyone who wants to come to him must believe that God exists and that he rewards those who sincerely seek Him."*

So it is important for you to understand that God is and that He wants to communicate with you. It is also important to understand that even if it is difficult or takes a while, God will reward you for seeking Him.

# I THINK I HEAR GOD TALKING

*Hearing and obeying*

The hardest part of hearing from God is actually obeying Him. Most of us have heard from God but discounted what He said as not being from Him, so we wouldn't have to actually do what He said. For me these were simple things such as, "Go and talk to that stranger about Me."

Of course God doesn't call anybody a stranger, but you get my drift. Here is the tough part: If you keep ignoring the voice of the Holy Spirit, He may stop speaking to you about that subject. So when I say, "No, that couldn't be God. He knows that I don't know what to say," I may be ignoring the voice of the Holy Spirit. Sometimes I'm sort of like a little kid sticking my fingers in my ears humming, "No God, I can't hear You… lalalalala," as though I don't want to hear God unless He says the things I want Him to say. Disobedience makes it harder to hear. The opposite is also true. When you obey, you gain confidence and a greater discernment of when He actually is speaking.

Years ago I made a major transition in how I did ministry. I had tried everything, especially when it came to witnessing. I had memorized every argument and debate to lead people to Christ. I passed out tracts, went with street ministers…everything. I did lead a lot of people to Christ, but I knew there had to be a better way. I had heard John Wimber talk about "doing the stuff," and doing "what the Father was doing." I wanted to do what the Father was doing too, being led by the Spirit instead of trying to make things happen on my own for God.

I prayed and told the Lord that if He would give me a divine appointment, I would speak. I feared He would have me confront every person in line at the grocery store and totally humiliate myself, but I said I would do it. I knew that my hearing was poor at best, compared to all the stories I had heard, but I decided I would rather try and fail than wonder what would have happened if I had obeyed.

## *Divine Appointments*

Driving down the road with a friend, we had just come from praying for someone where nothing seemed to happen. Suddenly, I felt an urge like God wanted me to go into KFC. I can't say I really heard a single word, just a nudge from the Holy Spirit. After arguing with myself for a moment, I asked my friend if he would like to go to lunch. He said yes, and we went in. He walked right up to the line, but I scanned the crowd to see why God had sent me there (if it was God at all).

Immediately, I saw a lady sitting by herself eating, and I knew that she was the one. I just knew that I was supposed to talk to her. But I had no idea what to say, so I argued with myself about whether it really was God who sent me. Finally, I approached her table and stuttered, "I know that you don't know me but, I, I, well, I kinda feel like God told me to come talk to you."

To my amazement she asked me to sit down.

After a few moments of introductions, she told me why God had sent me to talk to her. Her life was a mess. The night before, she had tried to commit suicide. When she couldn't do it, she turned on the TV to the Christian channels, but it seemed to her that the preachers were all saying that they were right and everyone else was wrong. So she prayed, "God if You are there, You are going to have to send someone to tell me what to do."

The next day, she took her own car to school (she was being retrained after a work injury). Then she went out to lunch, which she hadn't done in years. She was sitting at that table waiting for God to send someone to tell her how to get saved!

After all these years, this is still one of my favorite stories. Over a period of the next few weeks, she not only got saved, but she was delivered too! To top it all off, one Sunday morning during worship she just dropped her cane and walked to the front of the church completely healed. In response, her husband, who was suspicious of everything, fell on his knees and gave his heart to Jesus. Wow! Saved, delivered, healed, and her husband saved too!

What would have happened if I had won the argument in my head? What would have happened if I had decided that the Holy Spirit wasn't really talking to me?

Nothing!

The biggest obstacle I find in encouraging people to hear God's voice and obey Him is that they have tried and failed before. I understand that this is not as easy as it sounds. Oh, hearing from God is as easy as breathing; but discerning whether or not it is Him, now can be difficult.

One of the biggest reasons that discerning God's voice is so hard to do is because we have false expectations. We go from one extreme to another: Either we think we only hear God's voice through the Bible, or we think that everything we hear or think is God. Neither is true or correct.

## *Testing What We Hear*

Having humility is a huge core value for anyone who wants to hear correctly. Our hearing or seeing is like the apostle Paul said, only "in part" *(1 Corinthians 13)*. But you will never get better if you don't allow the "words" to be tested to see if they are from God *(See 1 John 4)*. Paul told the prophets to speak one at a time and "let the others judge" *(1 Corinthians 14)*.

The Old Testament instructed the Jews to stone anyone who gave a word from God that did not come to pass *(Deuteronomy 18)*. In the New Testament, we have the Body of Christ to help us learn. We no longer stone someone for missing it. We are all here to help each other hear better for the strengthening of the whole body *(see 1 Corinthians 14)*.

John Wimber taught me a lot about sharing things I hear from the Lord with humility. He said that it is seldom necessary to say, "Thus saith the Lord." In fact, he had a way of presenting what he thought was a "word from God." He would say, "I think that God has shown me _____, but then it could just be last night's pizza." Instead of presenting ourselves as some sort of oracle of God, it is often much better to humbly submit what we think we are hearing for others to judge.

I tell people that every prophetic word is supposed to be judged. I tell them that even if I came to them and said, "God told me," it is their responsibility, according to Scripture, to judge the word (not to judge me). By "judge the word," I mean that you test it to see if it is really from

God. We can test words by asking things such as:

- "Does this line up with Scripture?"
- "Does it reflect the character of God?"
- "Does it flow out of love?"
- "Does it exalt Jesus?"
- "Do I sense the Holy Spirit confirming what this person is saying?"

Sometimes it is also very helpful to separate a word from its interpretation. People may hear things that are from the Lord but add interpretations that are their own thoughts (and may not be accurate). Testing a word helps both the person giving the word and the person receiving it to learn and become more confident in listening to the voice of the Lord.

A young friend of mine was convinced that he had heard from God that he was supposed to attend a ministry school overseas. What he heard seemed so clear that he applied and was accepted, even though he did not have the money to go. As the date came closer, he even went to the airport by faith, expecting that someone would miraculously meet him and give him a plane ticket.

When no plane ticket appeared, he called me. We met at a local restaurant. He was distraught and bewildered. He just couldn't believe that he hadn't really heard from God.

As we talked, I had him retell each word and picture that he received. After hearing it all, I clearly bore witness in my spirit that he had actually heard from God. But it also became clear to me that he had come to the wrong conclusion. He was not supposed to attend the school, he was supposed to work there.

With new focus and résumé in hand, he applied and was hired by this same ministry. Within a month, he was overseas working on staff.

Scripture says,

> *"Do not stifle the Holy Spirit. Do not scoff at prophecies, but test everything that is said. Hold on to what is good"* (1 Thessalonians 5:19–21, NLT).

If every time someone says, "God told me _____," we automatically accept what is said as being from God, we create an environment with a mixture of both words (supposed messages from God) that are actually from God and words that are not. As a result, all words will become empty and lose their power.

In a culture where anything that someone thinks is from God is immediately accepted as actually being from God, it is difficult to correct people because they've "heard from God." When someone says, "God told me," and will not allow the word to be judged as to whether or not it was God, it is a red flag that immediately causes me to doubt the word. This is very frustrating for me. I cannot help them even if I can tell that they heard wrong. Often, people just come to the wrong conclusions from what they actually heard from God, but without humility they may miss the real message entirely.

Often when I am trying to discern whether or not I think that what someone heard was from God, I will ask how they heard it. Was it a picture? What exactly did they see? Was it a voice, a feeling, a dream, etc.? I will do the same when submitting something to others. I might say, "Well, at first I thought it was just me, but then the same thought kept coming back again and again. I seem to feel in my spirit that it is right. What do you think?"

Further, when you humbly share what you think you're hearing with people you know hear from God, you can begin to tune in to God's station better. Really, the best way to grow in prophecy is to minister with someone who you know moves accurately in this gift. It is SO encouraging to be listening in a group and hear someone else say out loud the thing that you "kind of sort of" thought might be from God. As you hear them take the words right out of your mouth, you will realize you were actually hearing correctly!

In a safe environment of love and encouragement, you can proceed to step out in faith and declare what you think God is saying to you. As you experience times of getting it right, you will gain confidence. In a safe environment, you can also get feedback when you miss it and learn from this as well.

A test for any word from God is, first of course, "Is it scriptural?" For instance if someone says, "God is telling me that I should divorce my wife and marry this other woman," the word was not from God because we know what the Bible says.

Sometimes we have to learn whether something is from God by acting on it. There is no scripture for, "Go into KFC." The only way for me to be sure was to actually go into KFC! The nudge from the Holy Spirit that I felt that day has since become very familiar to me. That nudge is like my wife touching my head, I know it is her even if I can't see her. I know the touch from the Lord; He is close, intimate, and never pushy. But I also know that when my life is too full, and my thoughts and affections are on other things, I can miss His touch. This I do know, He is ALWAYS there. There is always an opportunity to be His hands and His feet for people who need an encounter with God.

As you learn to listen, here are a few cautions. God is probably not the person telling you about all your friends' sins, that is just not who He is. There is an accuser in the world, and his name isn't Jesus. God probably is not the author of dreams of coming doom (the Scripture says He will not give you a spirit of fear). Most of what He says will be to build you up, to encourage you to good works, and to comfort you *(1 Corinthians 14:3)*. His words are powerful! Just think of simple words like, "I love you," straight from God! How would your world change if you really believed that the God of the universe was actually saying that to you?

# WHERE DO
# STORIES
# COME FROM

*Nothing like that ever happens to me*

Sometimes when I share stories, people will say, "Nothing like that ever happens to me." When I was a young believer, I felt the same disappointment. In fact, I felt somehow disqualified because I didn't have miraculous stories like the evangelists I practically idolized. Today, these evangelists are still heroes to me, but along the way I realized that they are just people like me. They were not born with more of something that I did not have.

I also learned some other very important lessons about how the application of time to any story changes the dynamic of the story itself. When I read a great book telling of the wonders of God and of His works through the great evangelists of the past, I often forget that what took me minutes to read may have taken them years to accomplish. Books seldom tell about the monotonous hours, days, weeks, or years leading up to the dramatic miracle. Even if one did, I would probably breeze past that part to the juicy parts where great things happened. I like the highlights, and my life always pales in comparison to someone else's highlights.

Anyone who wants to reproduce these great testimonies must be prepared for the "life" that happens in between these mountaintop experiences. Seldom do the books or testimonies tell about all the times of praying for people who didn't get healed or the stories of people who did not want to get saved. The stories don't advertise the struggles with finances just to get by or the times of frustration. They don't tell people about the relationship struggles and tension; the stories don't tell of the times of doubt.

Maybe some people leave out those parts of their story when they share because they are afraid that their struggle takes away from the glory of the victory. I disagree.

Many of the miracles I've experienced were preceded by a season of what I call "the dark night of the soul." There is a burden involved. If you want to burn with passion for the Lord, frankly, it is going to cost you. Often it is out of great sorrow that a burden from God is birthed. We live in a culture where most people seek to avoid emotional pain at any cost. And yet, sometimes experiencing the emotional pain of deep compassion is a part of the process of preparing the way for a miracle. If you are unwilling to pay the price, you will most likely remain on the sidelines wishing that you were the lucky one to experience the wonders of God. Don't get me wrong, no price we could ever pay could come close to earning a miracle. Jesus paid that price for us. At the same time, there is a process to positioning yourself to be in the middle of a situation to become the someone who is bringing the Kingdom of God to that situation, not just a spectator. Carrying a burden prepares the way for something good that God wants to birth in the world, and God is looking for people who are willing to do it.

## *MacLaren*

Many years ago, I used to pass a facility for juvenile delinquents called "MacLaren School for Boys" on my way to work every day. While I was never a resident of MacLaren, I had been a juvenile delinquent as a teen and had spent time in another facility. Jesus saved me from that life. I was a new creation. Before I met Jesus, I had no hope. He gave me a hope that was everlasting!

In return, I wanted to serve the Lord with my whole life. I'm not really sure where I got this great urging to serve God. I thought everyone who got saved felt that way.

So every day on my way to work, as I passed MacLaren, I would feel a strong urge to pray for the boys in there. This facility housed the worst offenders in the state, so there were murderers, gang members, etc. But they all needed Jesus. Every morning God would tug on my heart, and I would pray for boys who were locked up at MacLaren.

Eventually my passion increased to where I was crying out to God to send someone to save them! I should have seen this coming, but I didn't. One night at a prayer meeting, I saw a vision of the sign out front of MacLaren. I began to cry out with tears for God to send someone to do miracles and show them that He was real.

"Well," He asked, "how about you?" I quickly changed my tune. In my best imitation of Moses I tried to explain to God why I was unqualified for the job. I don't speak too good, I don't have time, I wouldn't even know where to start, etc. All my excuses were met with silence. I knew from His silence that He would not make me go, but I couldn't ask Him to use me if I wasn't willing to take the assignment when He gave it.

The next day I started making some calls. Every call led to a dead end.

There didn't seem to be any way for me to get in there. To be honest, I felt slightly relieved, but the urging in my heart wouldn't let me stop trying. I just had to go into the office and ask. Eventually, I was able to make an appointment with the chaplain. This turned out to be one of the most discouraging meetings I have ever had with a Christian authority figure. The chaplain did everything he could to discourage me from going. He told me how bad the kids were and how overworked the staff was. Even worse, he told me that the last thing he needed was someone coming in there and leading kids to Christ. I couldn't believe my ears! I was so offended by what he said that I almost dropped it all right there.

But then he told me there was a small group that went to one of the cottages on Tuesday nights for about an hour and a half, and if I really wanted to I could join them.

Well, I didn't really want to. Especially if I wasn't allowed to lead anyone to Christ! But by the time Tuesday came around, I had gotten over my hissy fit, and the burden on my heart made me go. There were about five really nice people who had been coming every week from Vancouver, Washington, which is about an hour away. I felt convicted because these people gave of themselves, their time, and their gas to come so far and no one from my town came at all. I lived in the same town as MacLaren, and I hadn't come even once before. They told me not to worry about the chaplain. He wasn't really that bad, they said. He just didn't want any religious nuts coming and making his job harder.

We went out to the cottage. All we were allowed to do was sit in the lunch room and wait. Each cottage had about 50 kids, and we could talk to anyone who wanted to talk to us. We prayed and waited. Eventually, a few kids who were bored with the movie that was showing came in just to see what we were there for. I don't really remember who I talked to that night. It was a young boy who had come from a messed up family and didn't really believe in God but was willing to listen. I told him about God and what He'd done in my life, and I asked if he would like to accept Christ. To my surprise, he said he would!

Now, you have to understand that to me, one person accepting Christ was worth everything I had to spend! I believed that God loves people that much. After we prayed, he was quickly wiping away tears so none of the others would see. God had really touched him! I told him I would buy him a Bible and bring it to him the next week. This, of course, meant I would have to come next week. I continued to go every week, long after my friends from Vancouver no longer came.

Each week, I sat in the lunchroom waiting for any boy who wanted to talk to me. Just about every other week, I would lead a young man to Christ. I had to create an account at the local Christian bookstore for all of the Bibles I was buying! I did not want to give away cheap Bibles. In fact, when I bought one of the boys a Bible, I had his name embossed on the cover.

It is important to note here that I didn't always feel like going on Tuesday nights. There wasn't much fanfare for my going; in fact, few people knew about my visits. During this time, I was the only one going. And often I didn't feel "good enough" or "spiritual enough" when Tuesday night came around. There were many nights that I felt like such a failure in my own life that I didn't think I had anything to give.

One of my most vivid memories of those times was of me standing in the rain, repenting for my own sins and crying out to God, "They don't need me, they need you!" and then walking in empty handed. This happened countless times, and it seemed that these nights were actually the most fruitful. A young man or two would come to me desperate for answers and receive Christ.

One of the things that God taught me at MacLaren is that a huge part of ministry is just showing up. If you don't go, nothing will happen. If you only go when you are going to be seen or when you feel like it, very little will happen.

After a while I shared with some of my friends what I was doing, and some of them also committed to going to minister to the kids at MacLaren.

One day a great opportunity came up. Nicky Cruz, the ex-gang leader whose story is told in the book and movie *The Cross and the Switchblade*, was going to be speaking a few miles south of us in Salem, Oregon. I thought it would be a great thing to invite Nicky to speak at MacLaren while he was in town.

Nicky was willing to speak at MacLaren, and to my surprise the chaplain was happy to have him come! In fact, he arranged a special assembly for all the kids who were not in lockup to come and hear him speak. Since most of the kids had never read or seen *The Cross and the Switchblade,* or even heard of Nicky, I rented the movie (and a movie projector... that is how long ago this was) and showed it in the cottage I went to. After showing the movie, I gave an altar call and five boys gave their lives to Christ. I kept that Christian bookstore busy with all the Bibles I was buying!

When Nicky came and spoke, he was frank, almost to the point of being crude. He spoke their language. Nicky told how he was the worst of the worst. Unlike the sanitized version of his story in the movie, he had actually beaten David Wilkerson almost to death. Nicky told the boys about how as David lay there bleeding, he was still telling Nicky how much Jesus loved him! This broke Nicky's heart, and he gave his life to Christ.

I will never forget his altar call: "We are not going to all close our eyes and just have you raise a hand if you want to accept Jesus because if you are too ashamed to let your friends see you, you won't last anyway. But if you really want this Jesus, stand and pray after me."

Thirty young men rose to their feet and boldly prayed to accept Jesus. What I had for so long been crying and praying for was actually happening!

After a while, more and more of my friends began to go to MacLaren to minister. Eventually God released me from my assignment there.

Sometimes I think about what would have happened if I had never prayed for those young men, if I had never "gotten a burden." What if I had taken no for an answer when I first called? What if I had quit going when everyone else quit or when I didn't feel like going?

I can tell you what would have happened, nothing!

Perhaps if I hadn't gone, God would have sent someone else. I'm not so important that God can't do his work without with me. All He needs is someone who will say yes. But to tell you the truth, I think the pickings are pretty slim on the number of willing ministers.

I remember a young man telling me one time that he just didn't really have a burden for the lost; he was more called to church people. His father, who was sitting next to me at the time, turned and said something that I will never forget: "Pray for them. You will get one."

People say, "Prayer changes things." From my experience, one of the first things prayer changes is me. It's as if I want God to make some cosmic effort for things to change, when really, all He needs is a willing person to carry His presence into those very areas that need to be changed. Then and only then can He do what we cannot.

When I was a young Christian, there was a musician who I considered a prophet to my generation. Keith Green was controversial in my day. Many claimed his lyrics were too harsh, but for a whole generation of us, they were nothing short of inspirational. Even today the lyrics to songs like *"Asleep in the Light"* come back to me and motivate me like no others.

You can find the lyrics to Keith Green's song *"Asleep in the Light"* online here: http://www.songlyrics.com/keith-green/asleep-in-the-light-lyrics/

Keith Green's passion and conviction calling the church to action *(example quote: "how can you be so numb, not to care if they come")* is part of how I became the way I am.

## Youth Center for a Dollar

When I gave my life to Christ, my youth group was on fire in ways that the rest of the church was not. I was nineteen and actually too old for the high school group, but I was a part of the group for a while anyway. Later, I started a college age group. I was still a new Christian, so I found other people to teach. We were hard core like Keith Green. My friends and I would go to a different church any night of the week that our own church did not have a meeting. We showed up at every prayer meeting and home meeting in addition to Sunday morning, Sunday night and Wednesday night services.

Our college group loved to worship and we would do it for hours. We went out witnessing together for entertainment the way that other people might go out to dinner or a movie. On weekends we'd go to the airport and grab dessert at a restaurant before we spent the rest of the evening singing and passing out tracts throughout the concourse. We prayed for anyone who would let us.

When I lived in Woodburn as an adult, the youth groups were a far cry from the on fire youth group I'd experienced when I was young. Woodburn is a small town and even though it had lots of churches, all of the churches were small. This meant that all of the youth groups were small too, often with just a few kids in each. Most of the kids were only there because they were forced to go while their parents went to a midweek service.

Now, to be honest, kids scared me to death. I was poor and unpopular as a kid, and I never learned how to relate to them (even though I had four of my own). Even so, I began to pray for the youth of our city. I wanted to see God do something powerful among them. I prayed and prayed but nothing seemed to happen. Eventually, God showed me a vision of a Christian youth center where the youth from all the churches could come together to worship, share testimonies, and get caught on fire!

Sometimes God gives me a burden for a miracle that feels like it might be too much even for God. This was one of those.

It is one thing to get a vision; it is another thing to know what to do with it. I had no money, very little time, and a wife and four young children to support. Still, the burden kept growing. I just knew that if we had a center, the kids would catch fire! I had no idea what to do, so I asked Tom, my prayer partner, to meet with me to pray about this once a week.

The first day we were supposed to meet, Tom brought three of our friends to help pray. We prayed and prayed. We also began to look for a location. It wasn't long before we found a small hole in the wall place where we could start out. It was in a bad part of town and even though the rent would only be about $700 a month that was still way more than we could afford. None of us had any extra money to spend. We ended up arguing, accusing each other of not having enough faith and all sorts of other stupid stuff.

Our prayer group broke up. The whole thing was dead!

Even then, the burden in my heart just wouldn't go away! After a couple of months, I couldn't stand it any longer. I was still no closer to being able to afford even a really small place, but I couldn't shake the idea that God had given me this burden to pray.

I called Tom and asked if he would meet with me again to pray, just pray, about the youth center. He agreed to come.

The night we met, our other friends came as well. We all cried and forgave each other. Then we began to pray for a miracle. We had literally no idea how it could happen. I made everyone promise that we would not do anything until we heard from God, especially that we would not look at any buildings for at least a month.

We met one night a week for a month, crying out to the Lord for the kids and for a miracle. We gave our all to God for this purpose, even though we knew "our all" wasn't anywhere near enough to accomplish the task. After about a month, my friends asked me out for lunch. We talked about our lives and families, but there was no talk about the center. I could tell something was up.

After lunch, they told me they had something to show me. I was wary, to say the least. They took me into a housing district on the other side of town. There in the middle of it was a huge vacant building. It had broken windows and briar bushes overgrown all around. One of my friends was a real estate agent and had noticed that the building was for sale.

My friends wanted me to lay hands on the building and "claim it by faith." I did, but I can't remember ever saying a more faithless prayer. It was just too much to hope for! Later that night, my friend called and said that he had gotten the key so we could get inside to look at the building. So we all gathered again.

The inside of the building was amazing. It was 30,000 square feet, with stone floors, two huge fireplaces, a complete commercial kitchen, an exercise room (with equipment) and a sauna. It was all just too much! They wanted to know what I thought, and I was afraid to tell them because what I thought was: "What are we doing here? We can't afford this!" Then they asked me how much I thought the rent would be. I started crying, "Thousands a month, I suppose…" I said, remembering how we fought over the impossible $700, "We just can't afford it."

The real estate agent kept pushing. "How much can we afford?"

I started weeping even more. "I just don't know," I cried, wondering why they would torture me like this when they knew how much the youth center meant to me.

Finally he asked, "Can we afford $1 a month?"

You should have seen the look on my face.

My friend explained that he had talked to the owners and told them that the building was not saleable in the condition it was in. He proposed that we repair the windows, clean up the building and that, just by occupying it, we could defend it from further vandalism. They agreed to let us have the building for only $1 per month. I fell to the ground and sobbed with tears of thankfulness to God. He had done the impossible, again!

But this is not the end of the story. Sometimes a vision from God requires more than one miracle to see the vision come to pass.

The first opposition came from some neighbors who started rumors about our new youth center. They claimed that if we were allowed to run a youth center in this location, their neighborhood would be roamed by drug addicts and gangs. They passed around flyers with pictures of broken drug needles, claiming that this is what would be found in their own front yards if we were allowed to proceed.

We were summoned to a special hearing of the city council to determine whether or not we could open a youth center in this location. People angrily gave their comments and accusations, and I was sure that we were going to get shut down. I just sat there and prayed. It was the only thing I could do. By the time it was my turn to speak, I was so afraid that I was barely able to share my vision. To be honest, I was shocked when I heard that the city council had ruled in our favor.

All five of us who had been praying together went to different churches in Woodburn. Each of us was able to find some friends from church to help clean up the place and get it ready. We were totally unprepared for what came next. Our churches, especially my own church, became suspicious that we were starting another church. They decided that they weren't going to let their kids come to the youth center.

Eventually, we were able to convince most churches to trust us. After all, we were tithe giving members of each church. If we were committed to our own churches, why would we try to start another?

My own church, the one with the largest youth group, refused to support the youth center for some time. It took six months for my pastor to request a meeting with me, seek my forgiveness, and ask what he could do to help. Sadly, by then our time was almost up. We only had the center for eight months. I heard that the property sold for over three million dollars.

I felt sad when the property sold and we had to close. The whole thing felt like a failure until I tallied up the fruit. During those eight months, we sponsored three evangelistic crusades with speakers who spoke at local schools during the day and at the center at night. These alone netted over 270 decisions for Christ. Beyond that, only God knows the value of what happened through the daily mentoring and encouragement to the youth of our city.

In addition, the friendships and camaraderie built between churches and across ethnic barriers (we had many Russians, Hispanics, and Caucasians) had a great impact on our city as a whole.

I would have done almost anything to see one soul saved, and God let me be a part of something that impacted our whole city.

The ministry at MacLaren and the youth center both happened because of burdens that God gave me. Sometimes I've carried a burden by myself (like the one for MacLaren), but more often than not there was a team, a few of us. I'm not always the leader. Sometimes I've gotten to be a part of the team that prays about someone else's vision from God.

## *New Life Rally*

One of the people God brought into my life to partner with me in ministry was Tom. I got to be a part of praying a vision God gave Tom into reality.

At first, Tom was just a customer of mine; he worked for a bank and ordered printing from me. When we realized that we were both Christians, I told Tom about Full Gospel Businessman's Fellowship that I had been a part of while living in Portland. We began to pray about starting something like that in Woodburn. After a while, we started a Christian businessman's luncheon. Most people just called it "Randy's Lunch."

Christian businessmen from all kinds of churches all over the area would come, but there were never more than 20 or so people at a time. We would worship, share testimonies, and pray for each other. Sometimes someone would bring a friend who needed Jesus. Lots of times, people who would have never come to church gave their lives to Christ after hearing the testimonies of a living God and His works in our lives today at our luncheon.

Around this time, Tom got really messed up (in a good way). He received the baptism in the Holy Spirit and began to pray in tongues in the back of my print shop. And Tom really went for it. Since Tom was an elder in his Free Methodist church, he had a key to the prayer room. He began to go and spend an hour there in prayer every day over lunch.

After about three months, Tom showed up at my print shop looking rather strange. Something had obviously happened to him. During his afternoon prayer time, he had a vision (Tom had never had a vision before). In the vision he saw himself and others who had become Christians, whom everyone in town knew, sharing their testimonies in an auditorium that was not a church. In the vision, it was like the whole city had come, including people who would never go to a church but were genuinely interested in what had happened to their friends who had previously been anything but Christian. Tom asked the Lord what to do with this vision, and God told him to come and talk to me.

Let me say something here, having a vision is not enough. The gifts of the Holy Spirit are not toys. If you have a vision and do not act on it by obeying whatever God tells you to do, nothing will happen. If you have a vision, ask God what your next step should be, and then do it.

I immediately bore witness in my spirit (sensed a confirmation) that this vision was from God and suggested we talk to our pastors and the other people he had seen in the vision. The pastors were not very encouraging. They warned us that it probably would never happen, saying that even if we found a place, no one would come. The individuals who were actually in the vision, however, were very excited about the opportunity to share their testimonies with the city.

Three of them really wanted to help make it happen: Skip Palma (the real estate agent who had found the building for the youth center), Tim Sturenberg (a recently saved druggy and car salesman), and Richard Butler (a recently saved alcoholic, brawler, and garbage man).

Richard was probably the most popular guy in the bunch. Everyone knew Richard. He was famous for the fights he had been in, for wrecking his Corvette, and for his drinking. If business was slow, bar owners would call Richard and offer him free drinks if he would just come to the bar. They knew that if people saw Richard's car, a crowd would gather. This, of course, usually ended up in a fight before the night was out. Now that Richard was saved, the whole town wondered what had happened to him.

The five of us began to gather regularly to pray. What else can you do when you get a challenge from God? We had no idea how to do anything like this, but we did find out that it was possible to rent the 600 seat auditorium at the local junior high school.

One night during prayer, I had a vision of a poster. In the vision the poster looked like a "wanted" poster, only at the top it said, "CAPTURED." Under the title was a drawing of Richard beating someone up, another of Tim with drugs, fast cars, and women behind him, and finally, a picture of Tom smoking dope. Under these drawings I saw the words, "AND SET FREE IN JESUS," with a picture of them together as Christians. The poster also had the place and time, followed by a list of names of other fairly new Christians who were going to share their testimonies.

During our prayer times, we were really impressed that we wanted unsaved people to come to our meetings and not just church people. We had people involved from almost every church in town, but they didn't need to get saved. So we put our posters up in restaurants, bars, grocery stores, and barber shops. Richard had the job of putting them up in bars; he quickly realized that he had to go back to each bar almost every day, as someone would tear them down at night.

When the time finally came, we had a New Life Rally in our town for five nights. No preacher, no famous people, just people from the area sharing their testimonies. There was also a young man who sang every night. He sang a song *"Ordinary People,"* that became our theme. (The lyrics can be found online at: http://danniebelle.com/music/dream/ordinarypeople.html). This song described that we were, "just like that little lad who gave Jesus all he had..." (The boy who gave the loaves and fishes to Jesus who multiplied them to feed thousands).

Each night, different people shared their testimonies; most of them had never spoken in front of a group before. Many of the people who spoke invited family members and friends who did not know Jesus to come to hear them speak. They spoke of intimate things like drug and alcohol abuse, marital problems, problems raising children, and their hopeless lives before meeting Jesus. Some even told of being suicidal and wanting to die, or even of trying to kill themselves before they met Jesus. They all shared that, even though they were not perfect and still had some problems, Jesus had totally changed their lives! They talked about how they were loved by God and had a reason for living.

Every night we gave an altar call for anyone who wanted to give their life to Jesus. Every night people came forward and were born again. Friends, neighbors, and family members all got saved. It was amazing!

On the last night, Richard Butler spoke. The place was packed. Richard was no public speaker, but, boy, was he entertaining as he told his story! He told about the hate, the fights, and trying to fill the void inside of him that only Jesus could fill. He told how it took his wife wanting a divorce for him to see the man he had become. He was just as passionate about Jesus as he had been about everything else before. He wanted every one of his friends, those who looked up to him before, to have what he had found.

Sixty people gave their lives to Jesus that week, and the lives of many who were already Christians were changed. Christianity was no longer a spectator sport.

Richard, Tim, and I are all pastors now. Back then, we were "just ordinary people." Actually, we still are!

Are you beginning to see it? Have you figured out why I keep telling stories? Are you beginning to understand where stories come from?

These stories started by being impregnated by God with a vision or burden. I think it is important that you have given and continue to give God your whole heart so that this can happen. There is pain and growth in carrying a vision God has given you. The prayer and travail to bring a vision to life can be like childbirth. As you pray you are changed, to where you would do absolutely anything to see the vision come to pass. Great testimonies and great fruit don't happen because a person is a spiritual superstar. They happen because people are willing to receive, believe in, and contend for visions that God puts in their hearts.

# ORDINARY PEOPLE EMPOWERED BY GOD

*Change your community*

When I first got saved and for years afterward, it seemed to me that every sermon I heard on Sunday morning was an invitation to accept Jesus. Now preaching the gospel is a good thing, but when, as far as I could tell, we knew that everyone in the room was already saved, I didn't see the point. During every altar call I remember praying fervently that someone would respond, especially if a visitor had happened to come that day. Sometimes I would hear those wonderful words, "I see that hand," and rejoice that another soul was brought into the Kingdom. But really, what was the point in preaching the gospel to people who already knew Jesus?

However, all those altar calls did have a side effect. Through them, I developed a deep desire to see souls saved. I took the Great Commission to heart. I believed that we truly have one main job while here on earth, and that is to lead others to Christ.

I also learned another very important principle: "The Dead Sea has no outlet." I've been told that because water only pours into the Dead Sea and not out, the water of the Dead Sea is good for nothing. It is dead; there is no life in it. We become just like the Dead Sea when we live for only ourselves. We die in our passion if we don't serve.

It doesn't seem to matter how much you get, it will never be enough if you don't give. It doesn't matter how good the preaching or how great the singing is if you don't share your faith; if you don't invest in others, you lose the joy of your salvation. Your faith then does not grow but loses its effectiveness, eventually rendering it powerless.

On the other hand, nothing will cause you to grow more than to serve others. I always say that the one who teaches a Bible study learns the most. The teacher has to study a lot more material than she will ever have time to share. In the same way, even a new Christian can share his testimony to others who don't know Christ and grow personally as a result. His testimony of "I once was blind but now I see," can truly impact his unsaved friends and family who have watched the change unfold before their eyes.

Since most new believers still have friends who don't know Christ, they lead more people to Christ than anybody else. New believers carry that "first love" that is so attractive to those looking for answers.

### *Billy Brown*

When I first got involved with Full Gospel Business Men's Fellowship International (FGBMFI), this was one of the main things that attracted me to the group. The founder, Demos Shakarian, envisioned smoke filled rooms where unsaved businessmen, who would never visit a church, would come at the invitation of another business associate and hear other businessmen (not preachers) like themselves share their testimonies. Demos believed that when these men heard about how God had saved businesses, marriages, and people, they too would seek Jesus for themselves.

More than one man was tricked into coming to a meeting by a customer, only to leave as a brand new person. Most were not tricked, but many were pleasantly surprised that the "product" was real. Every businessman knows that word of mouth is the best advertising. No matter how many times a preacher says something, it means so much more when someone not very different from ourselves can say, "It worked for me."

There was also a power element at FGBMFI. As I have often said before, "It is easy to lead someone to Christ when they just got healed." Usually not only the person who gets healed, but also his whole family gets saved when events happen that declare that God is more than just what some people believe in: He is real, He is alive, and He cares about you.

Many people try to water down this part of the gospel. In an effort to avoid being offensive, they try to act as much like the people in the world as possible; they don't want the unbeliever to feel uncomfortable. This has never worked for me. If we don't have anything different than the world, why should someone who doesn't follow Christ change anything? But let me tell you something. When they are in trouble, they will look for the "fanatic" who might be able to help. One of those fanatics who walks in the power of Jesus (and sometimes makes other people uncomfortable) is my friend Billy Brown. I met him on my very first visit to the FGBMFI luncheon in Portland, Oregon. And to be honest, when I met him, I almost left the place and never came back. I was already anxious about going to a meeting where I didn't know anybody. I had heard about it and really thought God wanted me to go. But I was only 20 years old, and I didn't know if they would accept me. I showed up early.

When I first entered the room, only a few men had arrived. One of them was a very strange looking man with a crew cut and glasses. He immediately walked up to me, pointed his finger first between his eyes and then at me, and said in the creepiest voice I'd ever heard, "God told me you would be here todaaaaay." I literally turned on my heels and ran back out the door, out of the restaurant, and down the street. Once I was outside, I began my normal wrestling with God. He was urging me to go inside, and I was fearful of what was going to happen. I waited until exactly noon to reenter the room, hoping that the others would protect me from Billy. When I walked in, I tried to stay as far from Billy as possible, but he called to me from across the room and pointed to a chair he had saved for me. Everyone looked at me, wondering what I was going to do.

At that moment, I heard the scripture inside my head, "*God has chosen the foolish things of this world to confound the wise*" *(1 Corinthians 1:27, KJV).* I felt like I had a choice: I could sit with Billy and be considered his associate or sit with the rich businessmen and be one of them. I wanted to be one of the rich businessmen, but I could tell that God had other plans. I went and sat with Billy.

Later, the group introduced themselves around the room. Each person would stand, give their name, and tell where they worked. They were doctors, lawyers, etc. When Billy stood he announced, "My name is Billy Brown and I pray." I was embarrassed to be sitting next to him. But after the meeting, it was a different story. All of these rich businessmen came to Billy for prayer. I watched him simply raise his hand, and a man across the room instantly fell to the floor (some call this being "slain in the Spirit"). I saw him pray for a man with back problems by command-ing one of his legs to grow…and it did! I saw it with my own eyes! Soon I was helping catch the people who Billy prayed for. From then on, I was considered "with" Billy.

Every week I would come and help Billy. I guess I became his appren-tice. I really wanted what he had. He gave me scriptures to memorize, in addition to helping him minister. Lots of times he treated me like his servant, but I grew to love him. Before long, I was doing all of the things that Billy did. People were getting healed by the power of God.

After a while, buying lunch out every week got to be too expensive. I realized that I couldn't afford to go to the luncheon anymore. On the day that I had decided would be my last lunch, a man met me at the door. He was waiting for me. I recognized him as someone I had seen from time to time, but I didn't remember his name. He asked me if I was too proud to allow him to buy my lunch. In fact, I was too proud, but I swallowed my pride and told him, "No, that would be okay." He told me that he had been praying for me and that he had a word from the Lord for me.

"God wants you to keep coming to the luncheon; in fact, He has asked me to pay for your lunch every week, if you will allow me." Of course, he had no idea what I had decided in my mind, so I knew this was really from God. I simply said, "Okay." Every week for a year, that man bought me lunch. There were even days that he could not attend but would meet me at the door and give me the money for lunch.

Wow. We have no idea how important we are to God!

Once a year there was a men's retreat for FGBMFI, and one of the men said he would pay if I would go. It turned out that he had also invited another friend who did not know Jesus, and the two of us shared a room. We couldn't be more different. I was a poor kid with more zeal than I knew what to do with, and he was a rich agnostic who really didn't know what he was doing there. A week before the retreat, he had experienced something that changed his life.

He owned a 55 foot luxury fishing boat that he used on the weekends to take VIPs fishing. On this particular week, a freak wave hit his boat and sunk it. Everyone on board was fine, but everything that he valued had just sunk to the bottom of the sea. He was a broken man.

Even though we didn't have anything in common, this rich agnostic put up with me. He didn't know anyone except me and the guy who invited us. During the second day, I saw some people praying for a man's leg to grow. I grabbed my new friend and literally pushed his head inches from the other man's feet and commanded him NOT to close his eyes. Within minutes, he saw a miracle with his own eyes. When he stood up, he looked at me in shock. By the end of the day he had found Jesus as his own personal Savior. Miracles have a way of cutting through a whole bunch of arguments.

## Woodburn FGBMFI

Years later, as I mentioned before, I started the luncheon in Woodburn, Oregon. After "Randy's Lunch" had been going for about a year, I invited an officer from the Portland FGBMFI to come talk with us about becoming an FGBMFI chapter ourselves. My friends in Woodburn got excited about the idea, so we decided to hold a breakfast meeting. We invited more of our businessmen friends to come and hear the officer from the Portland chapter talk about FGBMFI.

While the businessmen were excited, the pastors among us were not.

They were afraid that money that was supposed to go to tithes would instead be spent at FGBMFI. They were also concerned that I would be disappointed by lack of support since they had a terrible time getting any of the men in the church to volunteer for anything. They didn't think it would work in such a small town.

On the day of the breakfast, about 50 men showed up. All of them were excited to start a chapter of FGBMFI because all of them had friends whom they could invite to a banquet, friends who would not go with them to church. What happened next surprised me, well, more like humbled and humiliated me. As we held elections for our new chapter, I was nominated as one of the candidates for president, along with a couple of others. A mechanic friend of mine was elected. Then, I was nominated for vice president. Again, someone else was elected, this time a contractor from the area. The same thing happened with the offices of secretary and treasurer.

Wow! I was nominated every time but not elected as an officer for the very group I had started. I didn't know what to think. The group decided to add a second vice president, but the same thing happened. Finally, they decided to add a third vice president and not even vote but just add me. I really felt strange about the whole thing, but I also knew that the chapter wasn't about me. I determined to serve to the best of my ability. Something really powerful happens when men get together from different churches to reach their community for Christ. Men who were faithful in their churches but had very little that they could do, men who previously felt uninvolved, could now go to work. And work they did! They may not have preached as well as a pastor or knew their Bibles as well, but they could sure invite people to come and hear testimonies of what God was doing in their lives. These honest, hard working men were respected in the community by their customers and vendors alike.

Many came purely out of respect for the one who invited them. At the same time, unity was created in the body of Christ across our city as we became friends.

We started a monthly breakfast meeting, a monthly banquet, a monthly prayer meeting, and of course the weekly luncheon (Randy's Lunch). I continued to run the luncheon the same as before.

Eventually, pastors from the community started coming as well. We honored them. Sometimes we asked them to speak (they could always share a testimony like anybody else). The pastors could see that new people were being added to their congregations as more and more people got saved. Furthermore, people who had previously only attended church were becoming activated in their own walks with Christ. As the businessmen realized that they were ministers too, they became more active in their local churches as well as FGBMFI.

I became friends with many of the local pastors during this time. All of their schedules were busy, but they came to the lunch whenever they could. We prayed for them and their churches, often helping to carry the burdens these pastors carried when someone in their church was sick, etc. Pastors soon found that they could come by to be refreshed themselves.

Many of the pastors who joined us led Spanish speaking churches. I loved their enthusiastic approach to worship, witnessing, and praying. We did whatever we could to help them. We built bridges where there had once been walls between the Hispanic communities of believers and the rest of town.

There is also a large Russian community in Woodburn, and we became friends with them as well. I can't even count the number of meetings I had where everything I said was translated into Spanish and Russian.

I'm not sure how many people accepted the Lord that first year, but it was a lot. There were many testimonies of healing, and other ministries were being launched all the time. Soon some of our men went and launched a chapter in the nearby town of Canby as well.

The New Year brought new elections and a repeat of the previous year. Again I was nominated but not elected for each office. This time I got a promotion to second VP. The previous year's VP became the president of the chapter.

We continued to have monthly banquets, breakfasts, and prayer meetings, along with the weekly luncheon. More people came to know Jesus. One of my favorite things to do was to go out for dessert after the banquet with our speakers. We had some really incredible people come through, some were nationally known. I got to hear their stories; I also began to realize that they were just people like me. They had the same struggles that I had.

The following year, I was elected VP. I continued running Randy's Lunch. During this third year, things began to change. People acted burnt out. They also quit inviting their unsaved friends, family, and business associates to our meetings. Soon it seemed like we were just having church meetings, and we were all meeting'd out.

The next spring, all the other officers asked for a meeting with me before we had elections. They wanted me to be the new president. I hadn't planned to run for any office; my time was filled. They literally pleaded with me to take it. Finally, I told them I would do it but only if they supported me like I had supported them.

When I became president of the Woodburn chapter of FGBMFI, my well intentioned friends could not keep their commitment. Other things kept requiring their time. I worked hard to bring in the best speakers I could for the meetings but was discouraged when month after month, no unsaved friends were invited. Oh, we would still draw a crowd of up to 100 people to our banquets, but they were always the same people who, in my mind, were coming to be entertained.

At the end of the year, there was no one to take my place. I made an executive decision: no more banquets to lead people to Christ if no unsaved people were going to be there. I canceled the monthly breakfasts for the same reason. I kept running the weekly luncheon, but I changed it as well. Since we no longer had expenses for speaker's fees, mailings, etc., I decided to continue to take offerings, only now LUNCH WAS FREE. Every week I would make the announcement that if you could not afford your lunch, then you could just pay what you could or nothing at all. If you could afford your lunch and give a little more, your gift would be appreciated. I did this knowing that if I did not raise enough to cover the bill, I would have to cover it myself. I never had to pay a dime.

At this time, we were meeting in a small restaurant with a meeting room that sat about eighteen. As word got out, the room was soon filled with as many as thirty people. People stood, taking turns at the tables to eat. We would sing, share testimonies, eat, and then pray for whoever had needs. During this time, there were a number of traveling evangelists who would come by when they were in town to be refreshed themselves and to help pray for people with needs.

A number of the Spanish speaking pastors used this meeting as an evangelistic tool. They would invite whole families to the free lunch. Soon the restaurant was full of people who couldn't even get into the meeting. After the meeting, they would form a line outside the door to our room to come in to receive prayer. Often the line stretched across the whole restaurant. It would take hours to pray for everyone. It was a strange time. The first hour it would be mostly us old timers eating lunch and doing what we had always done. Then for hours afterwards, we simply prayed for people as they waited their turn. I still never had to pay a dime. In fact, it didn't cost any more than we had been paying to put on a banquet.

An average of five people per week accepted Jesus as Savior. Many of these used the free lunch as their own witnessing tool.

Even though people were getting saved weekly, not everyone was happy. Many of the old timers, the English speaking ones, wanted their old meetings back, where there were only 12–18 of us each week. They complained to the regional director of FGBMFI, so he came to attend a lunch to see what was going on. I didn't know why he was there but was glad to have him; he was someone I respected.

After lunch, the doors were opened for people to come in to receive prayer. (I really don't know why I never tried to find another location for the meetings. I guess it was because we had been asked to leave another restaurant when our singing had gotten too loud.) At any rate, the regional director helped pray for the people hour after hour. Soon his jacket was off, then his tie, and then his sleeves were rolled up with sweat running off his brow. He looked around the room; the floor was covered with bodies of those who had been touched by God. He looked at me and exclaimed, "Randy, this is not Full Gospel, but DON'T STOP!"

This did not make whoever had invited him very happy, and a few months later, while I was away, they had new elections. NO FREE LUNCH was their cry. I came home to this discouraging news. I was no longer in charge.

After seven years of having this lunch, I simply walked away. But I continued to print all their materials for free until they finally closed the chapter. I learned some important lessons during that time, especially about what happens when Christians join across denominational walls to reach their city. There is definitely a special anointing from heaven when we join with each other, regardless of what our doctrinal differences might be.

## Partners Club International

A couple of years ago this all came back to me in Sultan Hamud, Kenya. On my trips to Kenya, I was truly confounded by one point. There were probably more Christians in Kenya (83% according to Wikipedia) then there were in the U.S. There were definitely more churches. It seemed that pastoring a church was one of the most popular occupations.

When I would go to Africa, I'd have no shortage of invitations to come and visit different ministries there, but the invitations were not always because of my ministry abilities. You see, it worked like this: Every ministry was looking for sponsors; it was their hope that if I came, I would be so impressed with the work they were doing that I would come back to the U.S. and begin to raise money to support them.

The pastor who has the most support from overseas is considered the most successful. He has a car, a house, and many people looking to him for help. In that environment, it's easy for things like preaching the gospel, feeding the poor, and caring for widows and orphans to become tools to generate income from the states. Ministers all over the world pray and ask God to provide, but too often in Africa, the idea is that God will send a white man with money. Missionaries have been in Kenya for so long that many people just think this is how things work.

Now I don't mean to imply that every minister on the continent of Africa is a scam artist trying to raise money. Nor do I think that we should stop supporting local pastors in Africa. I have many brothers and sisters in Africa whom I deeply respect, and I am so proud to partner with them in their churches. It's just that I am aware that we may have created a welfare mentality within parts of the African church that causes them to look to people rather than God for provision.

This deeply saddens me.

When people get right with God, there should be prosperity. I am not a prosperity preacher. The gospel isn't some sort of "get rich quick" scheme, but I do believe that throughout Scripture whenever people turned to the Lord, He blessed them. He met all their needs and frankly, sometimes even made them rich. Even the crops showed the blessing of God by their increase. So why with so many Christians in Kenya was there still so much poverty? The crime rate was also high, and fear of losing what little possessions they had was common.

While praying about this, I met with a businessman and his wife and told them about my experiences with FGBMFI. The following year, I had a plan.

This businessman and his wife were both teachers who operated a hotel. I asked if they could prepare a banquet for other business people and if they could invite about thirty of them to come. They knew just about every business person in town. I could have invited more, but the $200 for the meals was all I could afford. I asked that they would get people from as many different churches as possible.

When everyone arrived on the night of the banquet, I asked them all to share their name and briefly how they had accepted Jesus. After dinner

I spoke. I told them about the Dead Sea; I told them about how God blesses when we join across denominational walls. Most importantly, I told them that they were all ministers of the Gospel. I further encouraged them that as businessmen and businesswomen, they especially knew how to "get things done." I talked about inviting unsaved business associates who would not go to any of their churches but would come and meet with them.

Many commented how even though they knew everyone in the room, they had never heard their testimonies. They all agreed that they wanted to start a Christian businesspersons group of their own. They elected officers that night. I was asked, as their founder, to return the following year to see their progress.

During that year these people went after it! They met for a banquet monthly. They incorporated their new ministry and named it, "The Partners Club International." They told me that they added the "International" because I was one of their members.

At one of their meetings they had an advisor to the president of Kenya as their speaker.

This is not my ministry; it is theirs, Africans reaching Africans for Christ. I am so proud of them. I know business people in two cities in Uganda that may very well start their own chapters.

What was my point in sharing these stories about FGBMFI? Simply this: people have to give. This is not an offering speech or get rich quick scheme. I am not taking a collection. This is how the Kingdom works. The more you give, the more you receive either here on earth or as rewards in heaven.

Giving of your time, your heart, and yes, your money is God's prescription for blessing you. If you do not give, He cannot bless you. He is the God who gave His very best for us, His Son. His children should be like their Father in heaven, giving people.

With that said, we really shouldn't "give to get." We should do it because it is who we are!

In the stories of this chapter hundreds of people got saved, a city changed, and lifelong allegiances were built because of ordinary people who were enabled by God to do extraordinary things. In the end, it was not about me. I was blessed. And the world changed.

You can change your world, too.

# IF YOU BEING EVIL

## Are you better than God?

I love to counsel people more than any other part of my ministry. But when I do, I find most, if not all of our problems as people are related to a misunderstanding about who God is. More often than not we just assume that He is like our earthly father, only even more demanding. We don't understand how He can have grace for us. We feel we must earn His grace, and we are hopeless that we will ever be able to do that.

When Jesus came on the scene in Israel, the people didn't really know God as a father. They knew Him only as a judge. They didn't know or understand His heart. Jesus said, *"If you had known the Father, you would recognize Me because I am just like Him!" (John 14:7, my paraphrase).*

We make the same mistake. I have heard people say many times, "Yes, I believe that God heals. I just don't know if He wants to heal me." That is like saying, "Yes, I believe that Jesus saves. I just don't know if He wants to save me." We would think the last statement ludicrous, but too many of us accept the first as a reasonable excuse for not having faith for healing. In Isaiah 53 (NIV), it says that He was *"pierced for our transgression"* and that *"by His wounds we are healed."* The wounds Jesus bore on the cross paid not only for our salvation, but also for our healing our complete wholeness. When I encounter people with this misunderstanding, I often use Luke 11:11–13 (NASB):

> *Now suppose one of you fathers is asked by his son for a fish; he will not give him a snake instead of a fish, will he? Or if he is asked for an egg, he will not give him a scorpion, will he? If you then, being evil, know how to give good gifts to your children, how much more will your heavenly Father give the Holy Spirit to those who ask Him?*

One vivid memory I have of sharing this passage is a conversation with a Hispanic woman. She was a mother. I don't remember her name; I only met her once. I don't even remember what her problem was exactly, but she spent a great deal of time confessing her sins. I only remember that she was guilt ridden and could not see that God would really do anything for her.

I asked her about her kids. She beamed a little in spite of the earlier tears, and she began to tell me about them. One of them had been in some trouble.

I asked, "Do you still love her?"

"Of course," she replied.

"How much?" I asked.

"More than anything," she said.

I asked her, "If it was in your power, would you do anything to fix things for her?"

She said, "Oh, yes, yes!"

I then asked, "Would you be willing to even die if it would save one of your children?"

She welled up with tears of love and responded without any hesitation, "Yes, I would."

"Are you better than God?" I asked.

A shocked look came over her face. Of course she didn't think she was better than God. Hadn't she just spent the last hour confessing all of her sins and shortcomings to me? Wasn't I listening? I opened up a Bible and read Luke 11:11–13.

*"If your son asked for a fish would you give him a snake? Or if he asked for an egg would you give him a scorpion?"*

She looked at me like I was treating her like a child.

"Would you give your children anything that would hurt them?" I asked.

"No, of course not," she answered a little less accusingly.

"Well then the Bible says, 'If you being evil…'"

Before I could even finish the verse, I noticed the hopelessness of guilt washing over her face again.

"That just means you being imperfect; you don't claim to be perfect, do you?" I asked.

"No," she replied.

"Well then, if you being imperfect know how to give good gifts to your children, how much more will God give the Holy Spirit or (in Matthew 7:11, NASB) good gifts to you?"

"Ah, I don't know," was her response.

I asked again, "Do you think you are better than God?"

Again, she said, "No."

"So, is it possible that God really loves you, at least as much as you love your kids?" I asked. A little light began to gleam in her eyes. This seemed just too good to be true, but she wanted it.

"Yes, I suppose so."

"So if you still love your daughter, even when she gets into trouble, so much that you would die to fix things for her, what does that mean about how God feels toward you?" I asked.

"That He wants to help and that He would do anything for me?" she responded tentatively.

"Yes, you're getting it! God loves you, He is on your side, and He thinks you are amazing."

About this time I saw a picture in my mind's eye of a little girl, about four or five, twirling in a ballerina's outfit. She was showing off for her father. In the picture, he was all smiles. You could say that she had him wrapped around her little finger, and he loved it. I shared the picture I had seen with her and told her this was how God the Father saw her. She left crying tears of joy.

If you only knew a tiny portion of how much God the Father loves you, you would understand that He is not the one withholding good things from you. This applies to every area of Christian life. God wants to bless you. He wants you to succeed. There may be timing issues, like my son driving the family car. I wanted him to be able to learn to drive, but not before he was fifteen. There were other adventures for us until that time came.

Am I saying that we have to wait until we're older or have learned some lesson before we can experience miracles? No, of course not. For some things, timing is everything. I think for healing, like salvation, the sooner the better. I just think that if you could see God's heart and KNOW that He wants to heal, then it would be a lot easier to receive faith for healing, as opposed to thinking that God is a mean judge who favors some people over others.

> *Who shall separate us from the love of Christ? Shall trouble or hardship or persecution or famine or nakedness or danger or sword? No, in all these things we are more than conquerors through Him who loved us. For I am convinced that neither death nor life, neither angels nor demons, neither the present nor the future, nor any powers, neither height nor depth, nor anything else in all creation, will be able to separate us from the love of God that is Christ Jesus our Lord (Romans 8:35, 37–39, NIV).*

If you could really understand who God is and how He actually views you, it would give you the courage to believe. Like the story above, it was not unreasonable to think that any mother would die for her children, but it was a difficult concept that God could love her even that much.

What about you? Are you better than God?

# THE MOST COMMON FALSE DOCTRINE

*"If it happened, it must be God's will..." Really??*

Religious people often explain harsh times as a punishment from God. Or they try to make sense of tragedy by claiming it is a gift from God to teach us something, because God is sovereign, and everything that happens is "God's will." Even insurance companies label earthquakes, hurricanes, and tsunamis as "Acts of God." The logical conclusion from this sort of teaching is that tragedy happens in our world because God wants it to happen. The religious way we treat the crises of life with statements like "God works in mysterious ways," etc., is just not right. It breaks my heart when something bad happens and people respond by saying, "I don't know why God is doing this to me!"

As I counsel people, walk with them through crisis, or pray with them for healing, the first thing that I teach them is that God really does love them and wants to help them. He is always acting for their good. Often just as people begin to grasp that idea, their faces cloud over and they ask: "If God loves me and wants to help me, then how come _____?"

I will probably make some people angry with this chapter, but it just has to be said. God is not in control. Now I don't mean that He is "out of control," or that the devil or anyone else threatens His supremacy. But I believe that the most common false doctrine (and the most harmful!) in the church today is: "Everything that happens on planet earth is the will of God."

> *Jesus said, "The thief [satan] comes only to steal and kill and destroy; I came that they may have life, and have it abundantly" (John 10:10, NASB, emphasis mine).*

Sin in the earth and the devil are the cause of tragedy, not God. Jesus taught us to pray, *"Thy kingdom come, thy will be done on earth as it is in heaven" (Matthew 6:10, KJV)* because His will isn't currently happening on earth the way it does in heaven. The fatalistic doctrine that everything that happens is God's will totally misrepresents who He is. For instance, I am pretty confident that in heaven, God doesn't give people cancer to build their character; therefore, He doesn't do it on earth either.

Jesus said that it is *"not God's will that any should perish,"* and yet He also said that *"the path to destruction is wide and many go that way" (Matthew 7:14, my paraphrase).* Is it God's will that any go to destruction? No! Yet many do. They make their own choice. God, who is in control, delegated the authority to men and women, who in turn abdicated that authority to satan. Now satan is called *"the god of this world" (2 Corinthians 4:4, NLT).*

The good news is that Jesus took that authority back. He said, *"All authority has been given to Me in heaven and on earth" (Matthew 28:18, NASB, emphasis mine).* His next sentence is a commandment telling us to go and make disciples, essentially, Jesus is saying, "I snatched your authority back from the enemy. I'm giving it back to you." Who is supposed to be in control? We are! Jesus commissioned us directly *"As the Father has sent Me, I also send you" (John 20:21, NASB).*

Jesus, being led and submitting himself to the Holy Spirit, did the will of the Father. In the same way, we are sent with the same leading and the same Holy Spirit to bring heaven to earth. We are carriers of the Kingdom of God. We are the ones who are supposed to invade this godless generation with the love of God and the power of His might. When men and women submit to God's authority (His will), then His Kingdom rules inside of them. When the Kingdom of God rules in a people, the very earth responds. The atmosphere is changed. Where there was once hatred, there is love. Where there was hopelessness, there is hope and faith.

Jesus sent His disciples out to the cities around Israel with the message, *"The Kingdom of God is at hand" (Matthew 10:7, NASB).* One way of interpreting that would be, "There is a new king in town and the rules are about to change." Then He instructed them to *"heal the sick, cleanse the lepers, raise the dead, …" (Matthew 10:8, KJV).* In other words, the rules of this King supersede even the very laws of nature, and He has come to reconcile you to God. This King is benevolent and He is strong. Heaven has come to earth!

Fatalistically claiming that everything that happens is God's will is like religiously putting God's name on the devil's own handiwork. We even act holy while we do it! This makes me very angry. I am jealous over God's reputation in the earth. I want the world to know who He really is. He is the lover of our souls; the redeemer of mankind. He is not some careless deity who, the only time we hear from Him, is to dole out some punishment.

We need to teach people to pray and ask God what His will really is in every situation and then submit to His perfect plan. I do believe that God is in control over those things that we submit to Him; however, like with Jesus, some people hated Him. They wanted to kill Him. They lied about Him. God did not make them do that, but if Jesus' life is our example we can expect trials and tribulations to come our way as well (see John 16:33).

Jesus never exaggerates. He always tells the truth. He meant it when He said there would be trouble. He also meant it when He said that He has overcome all the trouble in the world. God is completely able to work something good out of every dark circumstance. He can redeem anything.

> *"And we know that God causes everything to work together for the good of those who love God and are called according to his purpose for them" (Romans 8:28, NLT).*

# THE DEFINITION OF A MIRACLE

*Have you ever seen one?*

Many unbelievers have told me that if they saw a miracle like any in my stories, then they would believe in Jesus. (But because they haven't seen a miracle, they won't.) It is amazing to me how quick these same people can be to explain away anything miraculous that actually happens to them. It seems that some people would rather believe anything except that God actually exists and does extraordinary things.

For instance, I have read accounts of how experts believe that the Red Sea was only inches deep at the time of Moses, and that is why the Israelites were able to cross. It doesn't seem to matter that the whole Egyptian army drowned (by Egyptian historical accounts) in what experts claim was only a few inches of water.

So as we begin this chapter about miracles, let me say right up front that many miracles can be explained away by someone who wants to.

For an example, let's take a person who is desperate for money to pay a bill. If she prays for a miracle and then suddenly finds the money in a shoebox, or a check arrives in the mail that she wasn't expecting, she'll probably thank God for answering her prayer. She might even give a testimony of her miracle at the next church service. To the person who was suddenly able to pay her bill, that was a miracle. Yet it would be easy for someone else to argue that this wasn't actually a miracle at all, just a lucky find or a generous friend that made the difference. God wasn't involved.

As a pastor, it is my job to walk through the crises of life that each of the people in my church go through. It seems that needing a miracle is practically the norm. For me, seeing miracles is also the norm. You could even say that it is my job to be a miracle worker.

There is only one problem: I can't do miracles! I don't know how. But I do know a miracle worker; He is my boss (Lord), Jesus Christ. My faith for miracles isn't based on my ability or gifting. It is based on Him. I cannot dictate the "what" or "how" of what will happen but I can depend on who He is.

It was the same way for Mary, the mother of Jesus, at the wedding feast in Cana. She didn't know how He would provide the wine. She just knew He would. The hardest part of miracle working is that you have to believe before anything happens. Many have become discouraged in the faith because they tried to work the formulas. They tried to tell Jesus what to do, and when He didn't, they stopped believing.

I used to own a printing company. Designing brochures and posters requires a lot of creativity and imagination. It was not hard for people to make suggestions or critique the design after it was done, but as my assistant manager used to say, "Where were you when the paper was white?"

For me, this is what it is like to walk into a crisis. The enemy is declaring the worst. Fear and foreboding fill the room (which usually means that faith is not filling the room). It feels like an impossible situation. This is when I declare my definition of a miracle: *a miracle is anything that seemed impossible beforehand.*

For some people, believing that God cares enough to act on their behalf is a miracle in itself. The laws of nature and of experience usually trump most people's (even Christians') expectations. It is easy to pray out of our fear or pray a formula instead of asking the Father what He is doing and then pray for that. Many people actually "pray" their unbelief by dressing it up in religious phrases like "God works in mysterious ways." Or "Thy will be done." It's almost like they're looking for excuses for why something didn't happen even before they pray!

God is alive today, and He does care about you. He still does miracles. He still does the impossible. When Jesus calmed a storm (that had professional fishermen scared to death) with just a word, *"Peace, be still"* *(Mark 4:39, KJV)*, He demonstrated that the laws of nature were subject to Him. When He healed the blind, the lame, or the lepers, all of those miracles defied nature. And Jesus said that we would do even greater works than He did (John 14:12). In fact, testimonies around the world daily declare that God still heals and provides.

So what is the point of this chapter? If the definition of a miracle is *"anything that seemed impossible beforehand,"* then the hardest part of miracle working is that you have to believe that God is at work before anything happens. I am not talking about making positive confession, where we just walk around in denial, declaring hopeful things. I mean someone has to rid himself (or herself) of fear and unbelief and find out what God has to say about the situation.

In 2011, a close friend of mine, I'll call him "Charlie", was rushed to the hospital with appendicitis. The doctors performed an emergency appendectomy. This alone was very traumatic for his nineteen year old daughter, Janie (not her real name), who had just lost her mother the previous year. We encouraged Janie that everything was going to be all right. And in fact, the doctors came and reported that the surgery went well and that her father would be waking up soon.

Unfortunately, that is not exactly what happened. When Charlie first woke up, he was disoriented and became so combative that the doctors chose to sedate him again. All we could do was wait. With the loss of her mother so fresh, Janie was terrified. She asked me, "Is my dad going to die?"

Platitudes and clichés are ineffective during times of crises like this. It was a time of crisis, not just for her and her dad, but for me as well. After all, Charlie was my close friend. Even more importantly, I was struggling with what to tell her. She would feel a lot better if I told her, "No, he is not going to die!" That would have meant the world to her if it came from me. But God hadn't promised me that. And then if he did die, where would she go for comfort and what would happen to her faith when she needed it most? I could not tell her yes or no, only the truth that I didn't know for sure, but I knew that God was good and still did miracles.

Things went from bad to worse. Charlie didn't wake up. Day after day went by with him living in a coma, on life support. The doctors moved him to another hospital, hoping that they could solve the problem. In the new hospital, it seemed that every day brought a new theory of what was wrong. After weeks, fear was really starting to sink in. Creditors were calling, and Charlie had little or no sign of improvement. Finally, after a month, the doctors told Janie that she needed to be prepared that her father may never wake up, or he may live the rest of his life like a vegetable.

As she was giving me this doctor's report over the phone, I clearly heard from the Lord. I told her simply, "Everything is going to be okay. The doctors have done their best. Now it is our turn." As a church we began to declare, "Wake up" over Charlie, and the very next day…he did!

Why couldn't we have just done this in the first place? I don't know.

Miracles are not magic. God is not just a positive force like on Star Wars. He is a person. I cannot just wield the power of God when and how I want. I cannot make things happen "my way." Many times when miracles happen, there is a process involved. But here is what is important: Janie has her father back. The impossible happened.

These stories can go on and on. Another young lady (with a husband and two toddlers) whom I love was also in a coma for about a month. It seemed fantasy to say she was ever going to wake up. The doctors tried everything but continually warned of the worst. She was in three different hospitals having regular seizures while in a coma the whole time. As I talked with her husband, I kept encouraging him that God was at work. Eventually she did wake up and slowly began to regain her memory and cognitive skills.

She is now back at home with her husband and daughters, she even has a new job.

To God, the impossible is just the norm. He still works miracles for those who believe.

# THE NAME OF JESUS

*The name of Jesus is not a magic word
to get what you want*

In the Bible it says, *"You can ask for anything in my name, and I will do it, so that the Son can bring glory to the Father"* *(John 14:13, NLT).*

So this is what people do. They ask for what they want and say, "In Jesus' name" at the end of their prayer. Isn't that what the verse means?

NO!!!!!

I have never heard anyone talk about this, but it is one of my pet peeves. I have seen more Christians become discouraged from praying for miracles because of this misunderstanding than from any other. I have actually met people who asked for a million dollars in Jesus' name, and when it did not happen they left the faith, convinced that the Bible is not true! I met another young man who asked for the ability to predict cards so he could go to Vegas and get rich. He too left the faith when things did not happen the way he wanted.

The name of Jesus is powerful, and it has been lifted up above every name that has been named. But it is not a magic word. "How can you say that?" you ask. Let me explain.

In the book of Acts (19:13–16, NLT), we have this story about the sons of Sceva:

> *A group of Jews was traveling from town to town casting out evil spirits. They tried to use the name of the Lord Jesus in their incantation, saying, "I command you in the name of Jesus, whom Paul preaches, to come out!" Seven sons of Sceva, a leading priest, were doing this. But one time when they tried it, the evil spirit replied, "I know Jesus, and I know Paul, but who are you?" Then the man with the evil spirit leaped on them, overpowered them, and attacked them with such violence that they fled from the house, naked and battered.*

In this story they tried to use the name of Jesus as a magic word, and it did not work. The demons simply replied, "We don't know you." Our authority doesn't come from using the name of Jesus like a magic word. It comes from our relationship with Jesus.

When I was a boy, people commonly had an account at the local grocery store. Customers would purchase their groceries throughout the month and just pay at the end of the month on pay day. Even though I was just a kid, my mother could send me to the store (in her name), and I had the power to purchase whatever she sent me to get, even though I wasn't ever going to pay the bill myself. I represented my mom. It was her reputation of paying the bills that was in question, not mine.

As another example, imagine a policeman standing in the middle of a highway with an oncoming semi. If he simply raises his hand and declares, "Stop, in the name of the law," the semi stops. Why? Because the policeman is so big and strong that he can stop a truck? No, because the policeman represents the government that gives the truck driver the license to operate. The uniform and little piece of tin we call a badge identify the policeman as someone with the authority to command the truck to stop.

Jesus was sent by His Father in heaven. He said that He only did what He saw His Father doing. So you might say that He was healing and saving "in the name of the Father." He did nothing of His own accord, but everything represented His Father in heaven.

I visited Kenya in 2013. After speaking a message to a large church, I went and sat down; but the pastor of the church stood up, inviting anyone who wanted prayer for healing to come forward for me to pray for them. This should not have been unusual, as I normally pray for just about everybody when I go overseas. But this was a large church, and to be honest I felt a bit uncomfortable. About twelve people came forward. I went to the first lady and asked what she needed prayer for. She told me that she had a pain in her stomach. I prayed what I thought was a really good prayer (and yes, I finished my prayer by saying, "In Jesus' name") and went on to the next person.

But before I could ask the next person their need, I clearly heard the Lord tell me to go back and ask the first woman if anything had happened. Did she still hurt? So I did. Her reply was a very loud, "No, nothing happened and I still hurt."

Well, as embarrassing as this was, I knew that I would have to pray again. So I did, and then I asked her if anything had happened. Nothing had. Again, I prayed with no results. Secretly, I was looking for a way out of this mess. Even the congregation felt uncomfortable for me. I thought about telling her that sometimes these things take time or something like that. But then I remembered that it was God who sent me across the world to be here at this moment, and it was God who had told me to go back and pray for her again.

I didn't have anything new to say or to pray, so I told the Lord (which was probably just reminding myself), "Lord, I can't even heal a cold. You sent me here." I went back and prayed the exact same prayer that I had just prayed. Before I was even done praying, she started screaming and crying. She was healed. The pain was gone.

At this point, dozens of others who were sick or injured stood up and got in line to be healed. (It is amazing how responsive people are if they think something is really going to happen.) I continued the same method of praying until they received their answers. Every one of them was healed. Furthermore, for the rest of my trip, every person in every village church that I prayed for was healed. I had never seen this before and haven't seen it since. 100% results. Wow, was I blessed!

Why was everyone healed? Was it because I had discovered the "magic" formula, the perfect prayer? Was it because I have some special healing gifts? No, it was because I was sent "in His Name." It was really only when I recognized the authority that I was under that I had authority to do it. Jesus wants to heal and save much more than we want Him to. To become effective, we do not need to learn the magic words or special prayers. He has given us authority, the authority of His name, and we need to represent him out of relationship. When we do that, we pray what he prays and respond to His leading.

# DO WE NEED TO APPOLOGIZE TO THE PHARISEES

*Are we so unlike them, really?*

I n Sunday school, when I heard about the Pharisees, I thought that they were the "bad guys" who hated Jesus. I never thought about how much like them we could be.

These Pharisees were so committed to God that they studied and memorized Scripture day and night. Every part of their lives was ordered by their understanding of Scripture. They prayed many times daily. They washed ceremonially every day. Their diet was strictly established by their understanding of the law of God. They even gave tithes from the herbs they grew.

You have to hand it to them; they were really committed to God. Yet they missed the very One for whom they were looking. They were certain that they were doctrinally sound, but they rejected Jesus. He told them that they did not have the love of the Father in them. He told them that they didn't even know the Father; that if they had known the Father, they would recognize Him (Jesus). They were so concerned about religious purity that they missed the very heart of God, who He is.

In the first chapter of John, it says, *"He came unto his own, and his own received him not" (John 1:11, KJV).* And again, *"You diligently study the Scriptures because you think that by them you possess eternal life. These are the Scriptures that testify about me, yet you refuse to come to me to have life"* (John 5:39-40, NIV).

We, too, can miss it. For centuries the church of Jesus Christ has divided over doctrinal purity. Some sprinkle, some dunk, some speak in tongues, some do not, some meet on Saturdays, some on Sundays, some eat meat, and others don't. Each group has its scholars declaring that their way of believing is the right way.

Sometimes I think that the "religion" of Christianity actually keeps many people from knowing God!

I often wonder, if I was there, would I recognize Jesus? Or if I saw Him on the streets today, would I recognize Him? What if He didn't go to my church or to our Bible schools? Would I think his miracles were of the devil if He didn't talk my lingo?

The Jewish people of the day submitted as best they could to the laws of God. Being separate and pure were high ideals. But Jesus came talking about God as a Father. This was a concept that did not make sense to them. They saw God as a judge, a perfect and holy judge, who set standards that they could never fully live up to.

Sometimes today we do the same thing, setting standards of religiosity; go to church, read your Bible, pray, and overall be good. We can be so busy trying to live up to these standards that we miss who He really is. We avoid relationship with God.

The benefit of doing the right thing is that we don't experience bad consequences, but it doesn't build relationship with God. You don't even have to be a Christian to benefit and reap the rewards of following godly principles.

## Religion vs. Relationship

Religion uses fear, guilt, and shame from the pulpit to control and manipulate people into doing good. These are the very things that Jesus came to set us free from. Religious condemnation deceptively feels like a holy conviction.

It's like the little boy sent to the corner to sit against the wall. He says, "I may be sitting down on the outside, but I'm standing on the inside." Religion can cause us to sit and look good without changing our inner selves, but a relationship with Jesus will change us from the inside, causing us to be like Him.

Relationship is ongoing dialog.

*The Parable of the Good Samaritan*

*On one occasion an expert in the law stood up to test Jesus. "Teacher," he asked, "what must I do to inherit eternal life?" "What is written in the Law?" he replied. "How do you read it?" He answered, "Love the Lord your God with all your heart and with all your soul and with all your strength and with all your mind; and, love your neighbor as yourself." "You have answered correctly," Jesus replied. "Do this and you will live." But he wanted to justify himself, so he asked Jesus, "And who is my neighbor?" In reply Jesus said: "A man was going down from Jerusalem to Jericho, when he was attacked by robbers. They stripped him of his clothes, beat him and went away, leaving him half dead. A priest happened to be going down the same road, and when he saw the man, he passed by on the other side. So too, a Levite, when he came to the place and saw him, passed by on the other side. But a Samaritan, as he traveled, came where the man was; and when he saw him, he took pity on him. He went to him and bandaged his wounds, pouring on oil and wine. Then he put the man on his own donkey, brought him to an inn and took care of him. The next day he took out two denarius and gave them to the innkeeper. 'Look after him,' he said, 'and when I return, I will reimburse you for any extra expense you may have.' Which of these three do you think was a neighbor to the man who fell into the hands of robbers?" The expert in the law replied, "The one who had mercy on him." Jesus told him, "Go and do likewise" (Luke 10:25–37, NIV).*

Jesus mocked the Pharisees and the Sadducees when He told the parable of the Good Samaritan. To them there was no such thing. Samaritans were considered dogs, even though their religion was very similar with the same Scripture.

To put it plainly, Jesus placed a higher value on having Godly character than on having correct beliefs or belonging to the right group. To love is more important.

Knowing Him, to know His character, what He likes, what His passions are this requires more than a list of do's and don'ts. It requires dialogue and a heart submitted.

As the apostle Paul wrote:

*"I keep asking that the God of our Lord Jesus Christ, the glorious Father, may give you the Spirit of wisdom and revelation, so that you may know him better" (Ephesians 1:17, NIV).*

# GROWING UP IS HARD TO DO

## Lessons in love

I first accepted the Lord as a child at the Presbyterian church I had attended with my family. I asked questions during that time about the amazing things I read in the Bible. I wanted to know why they were not happening today. People told me things like, "We will all understand when we get to heaven," or "those things don't really happen anymore."

Eventually I lost interest, after I liked a girl who didn't feel the same way about me. I searched in many ways for God after I left the church. You might say that I became convinced that the church just didn't really know Him.

Years later, Jodene and I became engaged to be married. We were ready to set the date, and we wanted to be married in a church. Since we didn't really know how to go about it, we decided that we would have to go to a Sunday service to make an appointment with the pastor. My parents still received newsletters from my childhood church, and I had heard rumors that something had changed...something about the pastor's leg being healed.... But nothing prepared me for what I was about to experience. I got stoned the night before I went.

A lot of the people that I had known at the church were still there, but they had changed somehow. The pastor taught a message about the baptism in the Holy Spirit and told about miracles happening today. Then he went around with a microphone and let other people share testimonies about what God was doing. Some of these people were the same ones I had known before, only now they were talking about God like they knew Him. They told stories about healing and miracles and about hearing God talk to them.

One man shared that after receiving prayer the previous week for a bad heart, he had gone in for a stress test and had passed with flying colors. Another shared that after the church had prayed for her aunt with cancer, she had received a report that the doctors couldn't find any cancer and couldn't figure out why!

I don't know if I really believed all the stories, but I was so impressed with the changes I saw that I stood up as if to share a testimony and simply said, "I want what you have." Nowadays, I tell people that I gave my own altar call. Even though I had prayed to accept Christ when I was 10 years old, I still consider this to be the day I was born again. When I left the church that day, I was so changed inside that even the sky and the leaves on the trees looked different. I had a brand new start on life.

I was a new person. I would even tell people that the old Randy was dead. I approached my new life with passion and zeal; before, my life had no hope, but now I had purpose and the possibilities were endless. I received the baptism in the Holy Spirit, and He moved inside me with such a hunger for the Bible and prayer that I totally devoured my Bible and would stay up most nights praying. Within months, almost every page of my Bible was marked with highlights. I just could not understand why everyone wasn't as zealous as I was.

As a hippie, I had been searching for the meaning of life. Well, I found it! Jesus was the meaning of life. My car had bumper stickers all over it with sayings like, "Give Jesus a chance." I wore buttons with slogans like, "Not Religion but a Relationship with Jesus." My favorite slogan was simply, "Put Christ First," since my favorite verse in the Bible was Matthew 6:33: *"Seek ye first the kingdom of God and His righteousness and all these things with be added unto you" (KJV).*

To say that I was hardcore would be an understatement. If someone called me a Jesus freak or a fanatic, I took it as a compliment! As far as I was concerned, people who didn't give their all just didn't understand. One day in church, an older member told me, "Don't worry, you will come down to earth like the rest of us. Eventually, you will cool off." This was like a curse to me, and I vowed to NEVER become anything like him. I wanted to continue to grow in passion and zeal, not flame out.

In the college group, we pushed each other as far as we could. My friend, David Newquist, was the teacher at that time. We all learned to burn with passion for Christ, and we were willing to die for the sake of the Gospel. My wife was genuinely concerned that if they ever started persecuting Christians, I would volunteer. I soon decided that the only reason people did not want to become Christians was because Christians "cooled down" and stopped acting like Christians should!

Soon, it seemed that even my own church was content with being well... churchy! It was becoming more about religious exercises and less about saving the world. When they elected an elder who was unsaved, I quit the church.

## *Learning to Love*

Some friends of mine wanted me to start a church, one that didn't have all the religious baggage. It seemed like a good idea at the time. Mind you, I was only 21 years old, but I had already done more than most of the people in our church. It didn't take long for the people in this new church to decide that maybe their young pastor could use a little training. (I know! Shocking, right?)

They sent me to a spiritual gifts conference for pastors, which was quite an experience for me. Unfortunately, (in the area of spiritual gifts) I was well ahead of most of the pastors in this area. I found myself telling stories and well…bragging a lot. They were graceful with me, but any teaching coming my way was being ignored. I couldn't understand what they must teach in seminary. These guys didn't seem to know anything, and my head just kept getting bigger. Most of the pastors were from Charismatic Lutheran churches. I explained that my church was "non-denominational."

Just before we left, a man took me aside. He was someone I respected even though we had just met. He began to confide in me. He told me that he had never been to seminary, but please don't tell the others. He told me how his ministry had started in the parks. He was like a street preacher. He led so many people to Christ that various churches had asked him to come speak in their churches, and he became an evangelist. He had spoken in most of the churches represented at the conference.

But then he looked at me all prophety and said, "Randy, don't fool yourself. You are just another denomination." On the long flight home, the

Lord began to minister to me. Was I greater than Luther or Wesley? No, of course not. I began to see that even if I was successful in my new church, it would just become "the Church of Randy."

I went home and promptly closed the church. I still had a lot to learn.

What God did next seemed to me completely unfair. He sent me back to the Presbyterian church that I grew up in, even though many of the problems were still there, but God wanted to fix what was wrong with me. I had to learn to love. I had to learn to see what God saw in people, even what God saw in people who did not share my priorities. I had to learn humility, this would not be my last lesson on that subject.

After a year, God released me, and I moved to Woodburn, Oregon. To this day, some of my closest friends are from that church where I got saved. I honor the pastor of that church as my spiritual father. What a great honor for me it was to have him come and speak in my church that I started many years later. I felt like saying, "See dad? I did good, just like you taught me!" In fact, loving people (even more than spiritual gifts) has been my message ever since.

It is funny to me when now, as a pastor, I get accused of being the very establishment I was so against when I was young. It shocks me, so much so, that I have to do an inner checkup to see if it is true. Have I sold out? "No," I hear. I just learned love and respect. I learned to honor. I didn't slide into the muck of religiosity. I grew up.

Like I said, this wasn't the last time that God had to teach me a lesson about humility. Pride is such a killer, and religious pride is the worst! I am not nearly as dogmatic about some things as I used to be, in part because of a lesson I learned from an unexpected source.

## *The Christmas Dinner*

My print shop was part business and part ministry location. Everyone in town knew that I was a Christian and that I loved the Lord. Whenever anyone had a prayer need or testimony, they would come to the shop for prayer or to share. The Christian bookstore was across the parking lot from me, and rarely did a week go by that they didn't call and ask me to pray with someone to accept Christ or for some other need.

One day around Christmas time, a customer came in full of the Christmas spirit. Now, I was not the graceful man that I am today. I considered Christmas to be a pagan holiday. The Christmas spirit was something that needed to be cast out, not embraced. So fulfilling my Christian duty, I began to inform her about the origins of Christmas. I told her about how it was a Roman pagan holiday that just had the name changed. I told her that it couldn't possibly be Jesus' birthday and that nowhere in scripture were we told to celebrate his birthday. And for the coup de grace, I told her about the Christmas tree and read to her out of Jeremiah 10:3–4 (NASB):

> *For the customs of the peoples are delusion; Because it is wood cut from the forest, The work of the hands of a craftsman with a cutting tool. They decorate it with silver and with gold; they fasten it with nails and with hammers so that it will not totter.*

I told her much more than that! And when I was done, she left crying. I told myself that it was for her own good.

As I went back to work, I heard the Lord's voice: "Randy, what is the fruit of your ministry?" I knew immediately that He was talking about what I had just said to the woman. "But Lord," I cried, "I was right." All I heard in response was silence. After a while, I couldn't stand it any longer. I still believed what I believed, but I would try to do something Christian on Christmas.

Now, what was there about this pagan holiday that was Christian? I had to think really hard because I was so passionately against religious traditions that had no basis in Scripture. I thought about Christmas celebrations in my family growing up. Christmas was the time of year that we all got together. The Christmas dinner was always a centerpiece, and of course, the exchanging of gifts. Even if it wasn't all about Jesus, there was definitely love. "God is Love, that is Christian, isn't it?" I asked myself.

Finally I decided that for Christmas, we were going to invite someone to our house who had no family and share Christmas dinner with them. We still weren't going to have a tree or anything like that, but we would celebrate by loving someone lonely.

Only problem was, I didn't know anyone like that. I began to ask around to see if anyone knew someone who we could invite. Literally everyone I asked loved the idea and wanted to help, but no one knew whom to invite. People started insisting that they wanted to help. "I could roast a turkey," some would say, "or bake a pie." Before long, I had so many people coming over for Christmas dinner that I had to rent a room to hold it in.

But I still didn't have a lonely person to invite. You know, sometimes as Christians we try so hard to separate ourselves from the world that we don't relate at all with people who don't know Christ. I was becoming desperate. I called my friend, Tom. We prayed about it, and well, I kind of forgot about it.

A few days later the Woodburn paper came out. It was a weekly paper and I seldom read it, but someone called me and asked if I had seen the paper. I hadn't, so I went and got one. There, on the front page, was a story about my Christmas dinner. Oh my! NOW what was I going to do?

Soon the phone started ringing. More and more people wanted to help: The Lions Club, the Eagles Club, various churches, restaurants, and businesses of all kinds wanted to help. People wanted to volunteer and to cook. Churches had children's Christmas plays they wanted to perform. I had to rent an even bigger place.

Then a lady called me, all upset. "Mr. Conger, I am in charge of the Meals on Wheels in this area. We serve shut ins who can't get out of their homes to come to your Christmas dinner. We don't serve on Christmas, but I would like to help."

"Well, lady," I exclaimed, "you're in charge!" So now we were serving shut ins, too. Actually, that was great! Finally, we had our first lonely, needy people who I was confident would benefit from the Christmas dinner.

As the day approached, I finally had to tell people that I couldn't use anything else. We had more food than we knew what to do with. I took the money that people gave and purchased a bunch of little plaques with Christian sayings (you know, the kind they sell in Christian bookstores). I moved the location to the community center where Loaves and Fishes normally served people. The staff who normally worked in the kitchen volunteered to help me, since they didn't serve on Christmas either.

A lady from a local bank called and wanted to help as well. I tried to explain that I had far more help than I needed. I didn't even need money! I told her how I had purchased the presents and still had money left over. "We could wrap the presents," she offered. Sure enough, after the bank closed that day the entire staff got together and wrapped 250 gifts.

Finally, Christmas morning arrived. I had so much help that there was very little for me to do. I arrived at about nine o'clock. Many people were already hard at work. As I walked in, you wouldn't believe what I saw. There, dominating the hall, was a huge Christmas tree. It hadn't been there the night before. Before I could even consider how I felt about this, I heard the Lord almost audibly in my ear: "Gotcha!" He was laughing at me! The tree obviously didn't bother Him at all.

I know that many people will not believe that it was the Lord speaking to me, and I understand. I am not trying to create new doctrine or theology here. If you are passionate about celebrating Christmas, go right on doing it. If you believe like I did, I understand; you don't have to change because of my experience. I can tell you that I was changed, and my family has celebrated Christmas with a Christmas tree ever since.

Over 250 people came to dinner that day. Half were volunteers. Many were seniors who had no family locally. Some were poor families who would not have had such a great meal on their own. I split the volunteers up so that there were at least two at every table. Their job was to engage our guests, get to know them, pray for them, and choose a gift that was appropriate. During dinner, Christmas carolers and children performing skits entertained us.

The love and joy in the room was truly something to behold. Those who came as guests were genuinely grateful, and those who came to serve felt a deep sense of joy from serving.

As people started to leave, a group of young people came up to me, all excited, they didn't want it to end. They asked if they could go to the nursing homes in the area and sing for the people there. I gave them the rest of the gifts and encouraged them, "Of course, you can!"

Other volunteers went by twos to deliver meals to the shut ins. They did not just deliver the meals but stayed and loved on the people, gave them gifts, and prayed for them. Even after all that, we still had so much left over that I donated a bunch of food to Loaves and Fishes and about $700 to the food bank.

Unbeknownst to me, a photographer from the Oregonian (the state newspaper) was there, and the next day there was a double, full page picture spread of the people enjoying this community celebration. The next morning I was awakened by a phone call from a radio station in Portland, Oregon. The DJ wanted to know how I got the idea. "I was just trying to get over a bad attitude about Christmas," was my reply.

I hadn't realized it, but I had become just like the Pharisees of old. Doctrinal purity became more important than representing who God is. Love, joy, and peace are the fruit of the Spirit, and they should be the fruit of my ministry as well.

Why did I tell these stories? I'm trying to illustrate through my own experience, for people who are like I was, how I learned that passion and zeal and spiritual gifts are not enough. To learn these things was not compromise as I supposed. Rather, it was important to learn to see people as God sees them... through the eyes of love. I'm hoping that by sharing my stories, you can learn these lessons more easily than I did.

*Love never fails*

**M**any who know me, know me as the "signs and wonders guy." They know me because of the miracles they have heard about or experienced through my ministry. It feels really flattering to have this kind of reputation, who wouldn't want to be known for having the power of God work through them? Right?

That is, of course, until someone else needs a miracle and you don't have any in your pockets. Some people seem to think that I can just perform miracles at will. They don't understand that miracles follow me, like the verse, *"And these signs will follow those who believe..." (Mark 16:17–18, NJKV).*

Over time as I look back, I can see a steady stream of impossible things that have happened. But when I stand facing the impossible, I am as empty handed as the next person. Oh, I do have the advantage of having seen God rescue me time and time again, but I have to choose to remember this during the time of need. Love comes before any miracles or healing. Love is the motivation.

Actually, if I had my choice for what I want to be remembered for, it is love. I'd so much rather people said, "He loved me." I want people to remember that I believed in them before they believed in themselves and that I genuinely loved them and looked for what was good. In spite of my reputation as a signs and wonders guy, I teach on love more than any other subject in the Bible.

Scripture says *"Love never fails"* (1 Corinthians 13:8, NIV). I think the true definition of that phrase in the original Greek would be, "Love never ends"; however when all else fails, love succeeds where nothing else can. By not ending, love always leaves the door open for reconciliation, and the Holy Spirit remains free to work.

Danny Silk has written the book on what it looks like for Christians to love one another. I think his book *Culture of Honor* should be required reading for every church leader. Bethel Church in Redding, California has done such an excellent job of actually applying this culture that I love to visit and just sit in their coffee shop. No matter what I am going through, there is such an atmosphere at Bethel that makes me feel like I actually matter and that I have worth. I don't feel like I have to prove anything to anybody, and in fact, I feel like everybody there is for me.

Long before I had heard about Bethel Church or the book, *Culture of Honor*, I taught on this subject. When I taught people about spiritual gifts, I would tell them:

*The ability to receive revelation about another's faults is the lowest form of revelation. Even the devil will help you see what is wrong with someone*

*else. It takes a truly gifted man or woman of God to see what God values in someone with faults.*

## Guilt and Shame are Not Gifts of the Spirit

We, as the Church, have created an environment where people are so conscious of their faults that they lack the confidence to overcome. True prophets of God are those who call out the gold inside each of us. They proclaim the truth of what God says about us, breaking off the lies of the enemy and the curses of people who didn't know any better. Prophecy is the voice of love that reminds the sons and daughters of God who they really are.

Right after the great love chapter, 1 Corinthians 13, Paul gives the exhortation, *"Follow the way of love and eagerly desire spiritual gifts, especially the gift of prophecy" (1 Corinthians 14:1, NIV).* Prophecy is seldom the Jeremiah thing, warning of coming doom and judgment. Paul says in 1 Corinthians 14:3 that prophecy is for the following:

- Edification (to build people up)

- Exhortation (to encourage people that they can)

- Comfort (to remind people that they are not alone)

Proclaiming a Godly destiny can have miraculous results. Even the very least of us has a purpose and value. We are to honor people (see Romans 12:10, 1 Peter 2:17). Not just those who we deem as worthy, especially since none of us are.

All too often, instead of strengthening, comforting, and encouraging people, Christians try to shame people into improving their lives or to overcome sin and habits. This never works. Oh, it can work for a short season, but soon they fall back. The Bible says that Jesus came to deliver us from guilt and shame, so why would we ever use these traits as though there were gifts of the Spirit?

What's that I hear? You think I am one of those "sloppy agape" preachers? You think that people need to be confronted with their sin?

Well I do believe in confrontation, when done in love, that is.

## *Jesus Did Not Come to Condemn*

Let us look and see how Jesus dealt with sinners in John 8:2–11 (NIV):

> *At dawn he appeared again in the temple courts, where all the people gathered around him, and he sat down to teach them. The teachers of the law and the Pharisees brought in a woman caught in adultery. They made her stand before the group and said to Jesus, "Teacher, this woman was caught in the act of adultery. In the Law Moses commanded us to stone such women. Now what do you say?" They were using this question as a trap, in order to have a basis for accusing him.*
>
> *But Jesus bent down and started to write on the ground with his finger. When they kept on questioning him, he straightened up and said to them, "Let any one of you who is without sin be the first to throw a stone at her." Again he stooped down and wrote on the ground.*
>
> *At this, those who heard began to go away one at a time, the older ones first, until only Jesus was left, with the woman still standing there. Jesus straightened up and asked her, "Woman, where are they? Has no one condemned you?"*

*"No one, sir," she said.*

*"Then neither do I condemn you," Jesus declared. "Go now and leave your life of sin."*

In this story, Jesus is faced with a real dilemma. It was a trap that should have worked. The Law clearly said that a woman caught in adultery should be stoned (see Deuteronomy 22:22–24). If He denied the Scripture, they would have grounds to declare Him a false prophet.

Jesus' reputation was on the line here. He was known as a holy man, and yet He did not reject the naked, guilty woman in front of Him. He never scolded her. Instead, He knelt and wrote on the ground. I have heard it preached many times that He simply wrote the names of many sins. The Bible does not say this, but whatever He wrote had the same effect.

Imagine if He wrote the word "lust," how some who stood there staring at the naked woman might have been internally convicted by the Holy Spirit. Or "greed" or "lying" with the same effect. It also seems just too convenient to me that they just happened to catch her (and not the man) at the exact time that they wanted to set the trap for Jesus. Maybe He exposed this as well.

But He didn't even rail on her accusers. He didn't expose each of them, humiliating them in front of the rest. Though I am sure that they were beginning to think He would. He simply said, *"He who is without sin, let him cast the first stone."*

But think for a minute... why? If He knew their sin, why didn't He expose them? They had come to trap Him, after all. Why even risk it for this woman? I doubt that she was a follower of His. Was she worth it? He seemed to think so. She was why He came. *"For God sent not his Son*

*into the world to condemn the world; but that the world through him might be saved" ( John 3:17, KJV).*

He loved her, and the truth be told, He loved those who came to trap Him as well.

This kind of thinking goes against every religious bone in our bodies. God hates sin, doesn't He? Yes, of course He does, but He loves people.

## What Spirit Are You Of?

Check out this story in Luke 9:51–56 (NASB):

> *When the days were approaching for His ascension, He was deter-*
> *mined to go to Jerusalem; and He sent messengers on ahead of Him,*
> *and they went and entered a village of the Samaritans to make ar-*
> *rangements for Him. But they did not receive Him, because He was*
> *traveling toward Jerusalem. When His disciples James and John saw*
> *this, they said, "Lord, do You want us to command fire to come down*
> *from heaven and consume them?" But He turned and rebuked them,*
> *and said, "You do not know what kind of spirit you are of; for the*
> *Son of Man did not come to destroy men's lives, but to save them."*
> *And they went on to another village.*

I love the fact that the disciples thought they could actually call fire from heaven, but that is not my point here. *"You do not know what kind of spirit you are of…"* He did not come to punish sinners; He came to rescue all of us from the punishment that we deserve.

To hear some prophets today, you would think that God is angry and fed up with all of us and is ready to "let us have it." Jesus says that this comes from a spirit that is not the Holy Spirit. This thinking comes from hell (satan) and not God. Satan is the accuser of the brethren (see

Revelation 12:10), but he seems to get a lot of help from self righteous Christians who don't know any better.

God is love! To know God is to know His character. To be changed into His image is to be changed to be just like Him. The Bible says over and over that He was moved with compassion *(see Matthew 9:36, 14:14, 15:32, 20:34; Mark 6:34, 8:2–3; Luke 7:13)*. Jesus was a compassionate man. He still is.

Paul said, *"If I have not love, I have nothing" (1 Corinthians 13:2, my paraphrase)*. Love is the motivation.

> *If I could speak all the languages of earth and of angels, but didn't love others, I would only be a noisy gong or a clanging cymbal. If I had the gift of prophecy, and if I understood all of God's secret plans and possessed all knowledge, and if I had such faith that I could move mountains, but didn't love others, I would be nothing. If I gave everything I have to the poor and even sacrificed my body, I could boast about it; but if I didn't love others, I would have gained nothing.*
>
> *Love is patient and kind. Love is not jealous or boastful or proud or rude. It does not demand its own way. It is not irritable, and it keeps no record of being wronged. It does not rejoice about injustice but rejoices whenever the truth wins out. Love never gives up, never loses faith, is always hopeful, and endures through every circumstance.*
>
> *Prophecy and speaking in unknown languages and special knowledge will become useless. But love will last forever! Now our knowledge is partial and incomplete, and even the gift of prophecy reveals only part of the whole picture! But when the time of perfection*

*comes, these partial things will become useless.*

*When I was a child, I spoke and thought and reasoned as a child. But when I grew up, I put away childish things. Now we see things imperfectly, like puzzling reflections in a mirror, but then we will see everything with perfect clarity. All that I know now is partial and incomplete, but then I will know everything completely, just as God now knows me completely.*

*Three things will last forever, faith, hope, and love, and the greatest of these is love (1 Corinthians 13, NLT).*

This kind of love is not humanly possible. It comes from God; however, there is an unlimited supply available to every believer to love supernaturally. Consider yourself a pipe, a conduit through which God wishes to love others. You can never run out because it doesn't come from you, just through you. All you have to do is choose to let love flow.

When all else fails, love never fails.

## Moved With Compassion

During my trip to Kenya in 2010, I had a really bad day. I had already spent more money than I had to spend, yet everyone asked me for more. Worse than that, the last two places I had been, I had prayed for two people who did not get healed. After my trip the previous year, when everyone was healed, I doubted myself and wondered what I was doing wrong.

I also grew really frustrated with my hosts, who conspired about my schedule in Swahili so I would not hear them. They lied to another host and me in order to manipulate my schedule to be available to go where they wanted. On top of that, our car broke down (which I had to pay to fix), making us very late for a speaking appointment at a school. Nothing was going right that day. Eventually I had to hire a boda boda (a small motorcycle taxi) and ride on the back of the motor bike to my speaking engagement.

Needless to say by the time I arrived, I was having a hard time getting my heart right. Despite all that, ministering to these children is so easy I could do it in my sleep. The children excitedly hung out of their classroom windows when I arrived. The kids are always so appreciative of my coming (mostly just because I am a white man from America, something they don't see very often).

As we gathered for an assembly, in front of everyone a teacher asked me, "Could you please pray for a young man who has fallen sick?" I agreed, conscious immediately of my lack of faith at that moment.

They led me to a dark room lined with a ring of desks. I felt instantly challenged. Seated at those desks, the principal, vice principal, and some other school officials met me. I could tell during introductions that they were, shall we say, not as enthusiastic as the children. I don't think they were believers, and unless I had come to give them money, I was more of an intrusion than anything else.

A 15 year old boy lay in the middle of the floor, unconscious and trembling. I looked around the room, even at my hosts who had brought me. No one in the room had faith for healing, including me. They all just seemed to stare at me as if daring me to prove what I preached.

You must know, reader, it is one thing to pray for miracles after the Word has been taught, testimonies have been shared to build people's faith, and music is playing. It is another thing altogether to see miracles when there is no faith in the room, when your own heart is not right, and when the person you are supposed to pray for is unconscious!

I looked at the boy, and compassion from God filled me. I didn't feel any power or gifting. I just felt love for this young man. Even if nothing happened and they all labeled me some kind of charlatan, I was going to do my best for the boy.

Getting down on the floor with him, I reached out my hand to touch him. He immediately slithered like a snake away from my hand. Shocking! I had heard of this kind of manifestation but had never seen it before. His movements were so unnatural that I didn't even think a human body could move like that.

I looked back around the room. The school officials all quickly looked down at their books, and my pastor friends who had brought me looked away. I wanted to say, "Did anybody see that?!?" But I didn't. Instead, I laid both of my hands on the boy and asked for the Holy Spirit to fall on him. He began to move more violently and then to growl at me like a dog.

Again, I looked at the others in the room and declared, "This boy is not sick, he is demonized!" I pulled him up and commanded him to look into my eyes. Now I was really feeling compassion for this boy and anger at what this demon was doing to him. I forgot all about my doubts and frustrations and when the boy opened his eyes, I just knew that he could see the love of the Father in me. I also knew that the demon could see that I had all of the authority of heaven behind me.

I encouraged the boy that Jesus loved him, and then I commanded the demon to leave. (Of course the demon did not want to leave, and I had to repeat myself a few times.) After the demon left, the boy was fully conscious but a little weak. I asked one of the pastors to lead him in a sinner's prayer in his own language, and he was saved. Within 15 minutes, we were taking pictures together outside.

I later learned that the staff thought the boy had cranial malaria, a disease that people seldom recover from in the bush of Africa. They had already called his guardian to come and get him and take him home to die. What an impact the love of God had on that school that day.

God is just looking for willing vessels. You don't have to be great. You just have to know the only one who really is, Jesus, the lover of our souls.

What a contrast between living as a conduit for the love of God and living like a mere human in this world.

## *The Love Vibe*

I remember living in the inner city before I had accepted Jesus into my life. I would walk around with a look on my face that everyone in the inner city knows. It is called "the ghetto stare." Basically you walk around looking angry, and you never look anyone in the eyes unless you are staring them down. Everybody deliberately sends off the vibe, "Don't mess with me."

As a Christian, it is different. You look people in the eye, and you believe the best about and for them. You generally have a smile of greeting on your face. You send off a totally different vibe that says, "I have enough love and joy for the both of us." You communicate, "I am not afraid because I know that *'Perfect love casts out fear'" (1 John 4:18, NKJV).*

Never is this so evident as when I go to Africa. In my quest to go "to the least of the least," I often travel to places where they seldom see white people. The children run after the car, waving and yelling, "Mzungu, mzungu (stranger)." A simple smile from me (the strange white guy) brings them such joy. What power to be able to encourage and bring joy simply by smiling! Wow.

Sometimes I have dramatic stories, but honestly, most of what happens when I'm in Africa isn't the stuff that people want to hear as testimonies; in fact, I hardly know how to share about it. The amount of favor I receive and the invitations to make personal visits to homes astounds me because I really didn't earn it. I am amazed that people are so blessed just to have me come to their homes. I try to bless them in any way I can. I don't have much money, so I give what I have... love!

I was reading in the Book of Acts one day, and I saw this story in a way I had never seen it before:

> *Peter and John went to the Temple one afternoon to take part in the three o'clock prayer service. As they approached the Temple, a man lame from birth was being carried in. Each day he was put beside the Temple gate, the one called the Beautiful Gate, so he could beg from the people going into the Temple. When he saw Peter and John about to enter, he asked them for some money.*
>
> *Peter and John looked at him intently, and Peter said, "Look at us!" The lame man looked at them eagerly, expecting some money. But Peter said, "I don't have any silver or gold for you. But I'll give you what I have. In the name of Jesus Christ the Nazarene, get up and walk!"*
>
> *Then Peter took the lame man by the right hand and helped him up. And as he did, the man's feet and ankles were instantly healed and strengthened. He jumped up, stood on his feet, and began to walk! Then, walking, leaping, and praising God, he went into the Temple with them. (Acts 3:1–8, NLT).*

I began to realize that I have spent way too much time in my life telling God what I didn't have. In this story, Peter said that he did not have any money, but he was willing to give what he did have.

Of course, you may not be so confident to tell the man you have healing for him (even when you do). But as I read this story, the Lord spoke to me and asked, "Will you give Me what you do have?" This was not an offering speech, and for the most part, He wasn't even talking about money. He asked me to give away what I currently had instead of waiting until I had excess to give away.

Could I give a smile? Was that going to cost me too much? Could I love someone who no one else thought was important, even when I couldn't fix all his needs? Even if I didn't have money, would I do what I could, like go and visit and pray for people? The results really weren't up to me, but the going was.

Such as I have, I give.

## *Carrying the Love of God*

Driving down the road in Uganda one day, my host and friend, Pastor Hudson Suubi, saw one of his sisters near the side of the road. Hudson's father was a witch doctor who had so many wives that Hudson has almost 30 siblings. We stopped to greet her and say hello.

She invited us to her home for tea. I have seen closets in the states larger than her home. To this woman, to have me visit was as if Jesus Himself had come to visit. While there, I told her that another of her brothers had just accepted Christ at the meeting we'd come from. Her response? "I want that too!" and we prayed with her to accept Christ. Jesus had in fact visited her home that day!

We are called to be ambassadors for Christ. Just as the policeman does not stop traffic by his own might, we do not stand by our own righteousness alone. We have the opportunity to carry His very presence wherever we go. We carry the love of God. We can deliver His love to people as if He were right there with us, because of course, He is.

When I go to Africa, I go wherever I am invited that time allows. If I were to go to large churches in the large cities, I might not get the same reception that I do in a mud hut or a village church made of sticks. This is just fine by me; I am not there for me. I am more than happy to share what I have with those who really appreciate it. This works the same here in the states.

One day a young couple that would come to my weekly luncheon asked if I would come and pray over their new apartment. Only one problem, they didn't speak English, and I didn't speak Spanish. And I couldn't find an interpreter willing to go with me. I went anyway.

What a sight! There must have been twelve people living in that three bedroom apartment. Even more amazingly, they were so thrilled to have the "man of God" come to their home that they invited the whole apartment complex to come over for the event. None of them spoke English. I really didn't know what to do, so I just walked through the home praying over each room asking that God's presence would rest there.

When I was done praying, we met in the living room. I have no idea how many people were there, but everyone had to stand. They brought me a young man who needed prayer. Through their broken English and my very limited Spanish, somehow I was able to lead this young man to Christ. He was gloriously saved! The joy on his and everyone else's face communicated in any language that Jesus was there.

Then I noticed something that I will never forget. Trying not to let me see, they were taking up a collection of coins. I turned my attention back to the boy, and soon after they brought me a cup of coffee. They had raised enough coins to purchase a small jar of instant coffee. Now, my love for coffee is legendary; they knew this and wanted to bless me in return. I have never received an offering that blessed me so much. Even though the coffee tasted terrible, I drank it with joy!

We read about this kind of ministry in the Bible:

> *The Lord now chose seventy two other disciples and sent them ahead in pairs to all the towns and places he planned to visit. These were his instructions to them: "The harvest is great, but the workers are few. So pray to the Lord who is in charge of the harvest; ask him to send more workers into his fields. Now go, and remember that I am sending you out as lambs among wolves. Don't take any money with you, nor a traveler's bag, nor an extra pair of sandals. And don't stop to greet anyone on the road.*
>
> *"Whenever you enter someone's home, first say, 'May God's peace be on this house.' If those who live there are peaceful, the blessing will stand; if they are not, the blessing will return to you. Don't move around from home to home. Stay in one place, eating and drinking what they provide. Don't hesitate to accept hospitality, because those who work deserve their pay.*
>
> *"If you enter a town and it welcomes you, eat whatever is set before you. Heal the sick, and tell them, 'The Kingdom of God is near you now'" (Luke 10:1–9, NLT).*

I have eaten some things so strange that I didn't really want to know what they were. But to refuse would be an insult. In many places I have been, the people would have given me the very last of their food because they were so blessed to have me. It is awkward, but I must eat for them.

I am most amazed by the statement, *"Your peace will rest on them."* I didn't even know I had that power, but when these people receive you they do receive a touch from God.

## *Love Opens Doors*

In 2010, I traveled to Lugazi, Uganda. I have visited there many times, and I know my way around this town of about 20,000 people. Hudson doesn't like it when I venture out alone, but sometimes I do anyway. One day a woman for whom I had prayed at a church meeting the night before recognized me on the street and urged me to come and pray for her sick child. We went winding through alleys and houses until I was almost lost.

When we came to her home, it was kind of like a little apartment complex. Not wanting to give the neighbors any gossip, I stayed outside and she brought her son out to me. He was burning up with fever from malaria. I prayed for the boy, and when I opened my eyes, mothers from all the other units had gathered. They all had their children with them, and they wanted me to pray for them. So I did just that.

There was no need for a church service, no special music and no sermon! I just represented Jesus by loving people and praying for the sick. I could have stayed there all day, and people would have kept bringing me people to pray for. How easy is that? And how fun!

I learned that I can share the Gospel anywhere if I just love people and offer to pray for them. For some reason, many people have not heard (or shall we say seen) the Gospel shared this way. It is so easy to lead people to Christ when you meet them where they are and heal them.

I did this on the streets of Washington D.C. in the middle of the night. Now, I had been warned to walk in the middle of the street during the daytime, as the streets were so dangerous that people would pull you into an alley and mug you if you even walked close to an alley.

But in the middle of the night I couldn't sleep, and the Lord called me away from my room to pray. I was sharing the room with a number of other guys who had come for the one million man rally, "Stand in the Gap." The Lord led me to a park across from the hotel. There I sat, reading my Bible and praying.

Sure enough, before too long someone approached me and asked for (more like demanded) money. I only had like $20 on me, so I told him I would give him all I had if he would just sit and talk with me. I don't know why, but he did. I asked him about his life.

He was a homeless son of a preacher, who had left home long ago. His encounters with Christians had not gone well over the years, but he knew that he had a grandmother who still prayed daily for him. After a while, I asked him if I could pray for him. He said yes, and right there in the middle of the night, this tough guy started crying as the love of God washed over him. I then led him in a prayer to rededicate his life to Christ.

While we prayed, more people gathered. He introduced me as his friend to the others, and I began to share the gospel with them. About this time, one of my friends from the hotel came looking for me, very worried that something bad had happened. I just sent him off a few feet to pray with one of the people who were ready to accept Christ. We ministered to about 20 people in this way.

When we were done, joy and boldness so filled us that we just walked around looking for anyone else we could minister to. After a few minutes, three very big African American men approached us, and they weren't acting very friendly. They demanded our money. I don't know what came over me, but I just laughed (to their surprise). I was so full of the love and joy of the Lord that I simply replied, "Sorry, you are too late. I already gave away all that I have, but if you would like we will pray for you."

Again I don't know why, but the leader just looked at me with a puzzled look on his face and then said, "Okay, that's cool." I will forever have this picture in my head of that night with the five of us holding hands in the middle of a dangerous Washington D.C. street, in the middle of the night, praying and crying.

Love opens doors that nothing else can.

## *Edith*

Let me tell you about my friend Edith. Edith owns a very small shop in Lugazi, Uganda. She is a single mother of two children. She had not been treated very well by Christians and had experienced so much hypocrisy that she was jaded towards God and life in general.

One day I sat in her shop talking while waiting for a friend in the next shop. Edith and I chatted mostly about the United States and how she would like to go there someday, when I noticed a plaque on her wall that read, "What God says about me is more important than what people say about me."

I asked her, "So what does God say about you?" She said that she didn't know; she tried to be a good person but she really didn't know what God would say. I told her that she could know, that He really did love her, and He came to take away any sins or anything between Him and her. She gladly prayed and accepted Jesus.

This woman was a warrior, fighting through life in spite of people's opinions and judgments, and now she just met the creator of the universe and the lover of her soul. He would take charge and be in control from now on. I stop and see her every time I am in Lugazi, and I am so proud of how she has grown in Christ and become a light in her community. Again, thank You, Jesus.

## *Prayer Booth at the Oregon State Fair*

One of our pastors at Solomon's Porch, Gary Lewin, had a dream of having a booth at the Oregon State Fair, where we would pray for people. He loved fairs and especially the scones served at the fair, but he was really bothered by the long lines at the booths for psychic readings. Why should the devil have so much influence, and where were the Christians?!!

We rented a booth and created a sign that simply said, "May We Pray for You?" We did not advertise our church or preach at people; we simply wanted the opportunity to love on them. As a pastor, I was especially happy to see so many volunteers, who were normally too shy to talk with strangers about their faith, have the opportunity to see God move through them.

One of these volunteers was a young girl named Katie. Now Katie was shy, but always willing to serve the Lord in any way she could. She had volunteered to help with the booth, even though she had no idea how she was going to do it. After about an hour of her first shift, she came up to me and cried, "Randy, no one will let me pray for them."

"Well, we are just going to have to fix that, aren't we?" I said. I walked right out into the middle of the lane in front of our booth and grabbed three big boys and said, "See that beautiful young lady over there? No one will let her pray for them. Will you let her pray for you?"

Once they saw Katie, they were more than willing, but as she prayed, they got touched and so did Katie, her confidence grew and grew! By the end of her shift she asked me, "Do we have to be in the booth to pray for people?" "No," I told her, "you can pray for anyone anywhere who will let you." She proceeded to wander around the fairgrounds looking for anyone she could bless.

We prayed for about 1,200 people during those two weeks. We prayed and prophesied over everyone who would let us. We had new testimonies every day about people getting healed or needs met and some accepting Jesus. But one story stands out for me above the rest.

There was a young girl of about 15 years old. As she walked by, we asked if we could pray for her. She agreed because she needed a job, and she came back an hour later to proudly tell us about the job she had just gotten at one of the booths at the fair.

The next day she stopped by again to tell me more of her story. She was so touched that God had answered her prayer that she found a place to sit alone and just cried tears of thankfulness as she prayed and thanked God. While this happened, a lady (not from our group) walked up to her and began to tell her more about Jesus. She led her in prayer to accept Him as her personal Savior and gave her a little book of the Gospel of John.

She was a runaway, but after receiving Jesus she had called her mother and was going to return home. Her new job just happened to be going to a fair in her hometown in the next state, and they would take her home.

Now I don't know about you, but this kind of thing just thrills my heart! Isn't God good?!?

When we carry the love of God and allow Him to love people through us, there is literally nothing that can stand in our way.

Love never fails.

# EXPOSE YOURSELF TO THE GLORY

*Christians need to shine*

In Ephesians 1, scripture says that we are to be *"to the praise of His glory."* Jesus prayed in John 17 that the glory the Father had given to Him, He gives to us. If we are to be to the praise of His glory, and if Jesus is giving the Father's glory to us, I guess it is important that we learn just exactly what glory is!

Moses encountered God's glory in Exodus 33:

> *Then Moses said to the Lord, "See, You say to me, 'Bring up this people.' But You have not let me know whom You will send with me. Yet You have said, 'I know you by name, and you have also found grace in My sight.' Now therefore, I pray, if I have found grace in Your sight, show me now Your way, that I may know You and that I may find grace in Your sight. And consider that this nation is Your people."*
>
> *And He said, "My Presence will go with you, and I will give you rest."*

*Then he said to Him, "If Your Presence does not go with us, do not bring us up from here. For how then will it be known that Your people and I have found grace in Your sight, except You go with us? So we shall be separate, Your people and I, from all the people who are upon the face of the earth."*

*So the Lord said to Moses, "I will also do this thing that you have spoken; for you have found grace in My sight, and I know you by name."*

*And he said, "Please, show me Your glory."*

*Then He said, "I will make all My goodness pass before you, and I will proclaim the name of the Lord before you. I will be gracious to whom I will be gracious, and I will have compassion on whom I will have compassion." But He said, "You cannot see My face; for no man shall see Me, and live." And the Lord said, "Here is a place by Me, and you shall stand on the rock. So it shall be, while My glory passes by, that I will put you in the cleft of the rock, and will cover you with My hand while I pass by. Then I will take away My hand, and you shall see My back; but My face shall not be seen" (Exodus 33:12–23, NKJV).*

I just had to include the whole story....

The glory of the Lord is His very essence. When we gaze in awe at the beauty of creation, it is a portion His glory that we see. When we observe uncommon acts of kindness or mercy, it is His glory displayed. When Moses asked to see God's glory, God said He would let His goodness pass before Moses. God's goodness and His glory are inseparable.

In today's world, few people know how to recognize the presence of God, let alone His glory! And yet a noticeable difference should exist between the people of God and the people of the world. As Moses so clearly states, *"For how then will it be known that Your people and I have found grace in Your sight, except You go with us?"* Even people of other religions can be recognized by their rules. As Christians, we are supposed to be marked by the atmosphere that we bring, His presence and His glory, which looks like His love, joy, and peace.

God's presence and His glory, I don't even know how to separate the two. I am overwhelmed by this story in Exodus 33. The desire of God's people for generations was to enter into the Promised Land, the ultimate answer to prayer: a land of their own, and not just any land but a land flowing with milk and honey.

How many got discouraged and gave up? How many died having not received the promise? Yet here we have Moses saying, *"If Your Presence does not go with us, do not bring us up from here."* In other words, "Lord, if it is a choice between having You or having my prayers answered, I would rather have You."

Wow, no wonder God loved that man! But Moses didn't stop there! When God said He would go, Moses saw the opportunity for more, and he went for it! He said, *"Please show me Your glory."*

You would think that meeting with God would be so scary that Moses would get out while the getting was good. But no, not old Mo! He wanted to see how far he could go. I really think that there is something in God's nature that invites risk.

This same thing happens sometimes with little kids at church. Others tend to treat authority figures with an extra amount of respect, but little children will come right up to me (the pastor). They are able to discern that I am harmless and often just crawl up into my lap.

I think that those little children illustrate what Moses did, he wanted to get as close to God as was humanly possible. I think God wanted that, too. However, as Moses got closer, something happened to him that changed him even visibly! In the next chapter, Exodus 34, we read:

## *The Shining Face of Moses*

> *Now it was so, when Moses came down from Mount Sinai (and the two tablets of the Testimony were in Moses' hand when he came down from the mountain), that Moses did not know that the skin of his face shone while he talked with Him. So when Aaron and all the children of Israel saw Moses, behold, the skin of his face shone, and they were afraid to come near him. Then Moses called to them, and Aaron and all the rulers of the congregation returned to him; and Moses talked with them. Afterward all the children of Israel came near, and he gave them as commandments all that the Lord had spoken with him on Mount Sinai. And when Moses had finished speaking with them, he put a veil on his face. But whenever Moses went in before the Lord to speak with Him, he would take the veil off until he came out; and he would come out and speak to the children of Israel whatever he had been commanded. And whenever the children of Israel saw the face of Moses, that the skin of Moses' face shone, then Moses would put the veil on his face again, until he went in to speak with Him (Exodus 34:29–35, NKJV).*

The face of Moses shone, it glowed, a bright light came out of him. There was something about his encounter with the glory of the Lord that literally transformed him. The same thing happened to Jesus on the Mount of Transfiguration:

*About eight days after Jesus said this, he took Peter, John and James with him and went up onto a mountain to pray. As he was praying, the appearance of his face changed, and his clothes became as bright as a flash of lightning. Two men, Moses and Elijah, appeared in glorious splendor, talking with Jesus. They spoke about his departure, which he was about to bring to fulfillment at Jerusalem. Peter and his companions were very sleepy, but when they became fully awake, they saw his glory and the two men standing with him" (Luke 9:28–32, NIV),*

Literally, being exposed to the glory of God changes us. It changes us in very real ways. I have never seen anyone shine, but I hope to someday.

Just as Jesus prayed:

*I have given them the glory that you gave me, that they may be one as we are one, I in them and you in me, so that they may be brought to complete unity. Then the world will know that you sent me and have loved them even as you have loved me.*

*Father, I want those you have given me to be with me where I am, and to see my glory, the glory you have given me because you loved me before the creation of the world (John 17:22–24, NIV).*

This became very important to me when I had an encounter with the Lord, when He talked to me about how Christians need to shine.

I had traveled to India to represent a member of my church at a conference of house church planters from all around the world. The testimonies I heard and witnessed there were nothing short of amazing! This movement had over one million people coming to Christ per year in India alone. I was thrilled to meet normal people who were expanding the Kingdom at such an amazing rate, all without church buildings or clergy of any kind. I asked one old lady, who had trained thousands of women in prayer walking, to teach me what they did. She taught me about prayer walking, binding and loosing, and looking for "a man of peace." The Luke 10 teaching was so basic and simple, I was ashamed that I had not been doing it.

The next day we went out to practice. I went with a contingent of Chinese house church leaders (who had documented as many new believers as India had), and we traveled to major Muslim and Hindu sites. We walked around and prayed. At the end of the day, we went to a mosque. I was told that Muslim meant submitted to God, and so when I was asked if I was Muslim (submitted to God), I said yes. I went in to pray, and kneeling as they do, without shoes, I prayed for the salvation of all Muslims, that they would know the love of God for themselves.

Afterwards we were supposed to meet outside. As I waited outside the mosque, looking out over the mass of humanity, I was caught up in a trance by the Lord. (I have only had this happen one other time in my life, so of course it was very significant.) My friend evidently could tell something was happening because he kept asking me what was going on and what I had heard.

The only words I could find were, "To reach the world, Christians are going to have to shine." This was before I had ever thought about what had happened to Jesus and Moses. So at the time, to me it only meant that we needed to be changed in visible ways so that the world could see God.

The Apostle Paul wrote,

> *"But we all, with unveiled face, beholding as in a mirror the glory of the Lord, are being transformed into the same image from glory*

*to glory, just as by the Spirit of the Lord"* (2 Corinthians 3:18, NKJV).

Christians who are changed by God are attractive. Inner joy, love, peace, and confidence in any situation (let alone power to heal and work miracles) are traits that everybody wants. These Christians are magnetic and powerful, and these qualities are a natural outflow of time spent in the presence of God, drawing close to His glory. When we shine with the love and power of God, we see supernatural results that only God can do to draw many to want to be born again!

I find that the Muslims I meet overseas often have more confidence in Christian prayers than they do in their own. On one trip to Africa, I was invited to the home of a member of parliament in Uganda. The man was a Muslim, and yet he specifically asked for me to come to pray for him and his family.

The world is hungry for everything that Jesus is, if they could just see that He is real. For most of the world, we are the only evidence that they will ever have. If all we bring is scriptural references and a list of guidelines for how to live their lives, that is not enough; they already have rules and holy books in their own religion. To argue that our way is right and their way is wrong, based on our version of the truth, is just the stuff that wars are made of. The world needs to see bright and shining Christians who are daily experiencing the Living God and showing the true fruit that comes from abiding in Him.

Some of you might be reading this and thinking: "I'm doing the best I can to live for God, but I don't know how to shine or do miracles. Do I just need to try harder? Am I doing something wrong?" If that's you, first of all, I want to thank you for trying. Sincerely! I mean it! But there is a better way. You see, none of us can produce Godly fruit inside ourselves for God. That is God's job. He produces that fruit in us. When we try (no matter how hard) to create godly fruit, the best we can do is a cheap imitation. "What fruit?" you say. Love, joy, peace, patience, kindness, etc. These are the fruit of the Spirit, not our effort. They are the natural results of being continually exposed to the glory of the Lord.

## Teaching Children about the Glory

Every year when I come home from Africa, it is the children that I miss the most. They are all poor and many of them are orphans who face huge challenges of safety, food, and education. I just don't have enough money to help more than a few of them. I ponder and pray, "What can I do to help these young friends?"

In Sultan Hamud, Kenya, I met a young pastor and his wife. They took me to see their church building. It was just a one room tin shack in the poorest part of town.

While I was there, I was mobbed by children. I was told that they were street kids. This doesn't necessarily mean that they were orphans, though some may have been. They were just the kids of the neighborhood, who had nowhere else to go. I determined that in spite of my lack of finances, I had to do something. I planned a banquet for these street kids.

Now I knew that, though appreciated, one meal was not going to solve all their problems. Only Jesus could solve their problems and meet their needs. But I also knew that they needed to do more than just raise their hands and pray a prayer. These kids, and all of the kids that I would minister to, needed to be daily refreshed by the love and hope of God. They needed to know how to receive from Him after I was gone.

I would have bought Bibles for all of them if I could have afforded it, but I couldn't. You see, I am not very good at raising funds for my trips. I seldom get enough support even for my travel expenses, but I never have any problems raising money to feed poor children or people in hospitals.

As I prayed, I had an idea. I looked on the internet and found a source for glow in the dark crosses like I had when I was young. These simple crosses would glow in the dark after being exposed to light. They also had an inscription: "God Loves You." I bought 300 of them.

When I got to Sultan Hamud, I set up the banquet. About a hundred children came. They were not starving, but probably none of them had ever eaten a meal like this. They sang and danced for me, and then it was my time to speak. I told them about Moses and the glory.

I told them that when Moses was exposed to the glory of God, he was changed. I told them that in the same way, if they would take their cross and hold it up to the light, it would glow in the dark. I told them that they were just like Moses and the little cross, that if they would spend time with God, they would be changed. But I told them that after a while the light coming from the cross would grow dim, and it would need to be held up to the light again. In the same way, they needed to daily expose themselves to the goodness of God so that they, too, would glow in the darkness of hard times.

I gave an invitation to accept Jesus as their personal Savior, and six children accepted Christ for the first time. Then I got down on the dirt floor, hugged every child, prayed for them, and gave them the little crosses.

The same thing I told those kids on a dirt floor in Africa is true for you. If you will spend time in the presence of God, He will change you. He will fill you with light and it will shine brightly, changing the world around you.

Sometimes allowing the love of God to shine through you speaks even louder than miracles.

Later, while everyone was eating, they brought me a little girl who was sick. (She is the one pictured with me on the cover of this book.) They said that she had malaria in her stomach. She was crying. On my previous trip to this area, everyone I prayed for got healed, but for some reason this little girl just didn't seem to get better. I prayed over and over.

Finally, I just held her as she cried. I held her for over an hour, just loving on her as everyone else celebrated. Eventually she got better, but I don't think, in this case, it will be the healing that she remembers. I think that she will remember the white stranger who loved her and told her that God is love. I know that I will never forget her. When I got home, the Lord told me that when I sat and held that little girl who didn't immediately get healed, that was His favorite part of the trip.

On this same trip I found a stone at a school, painted as follows: "Be the change that you wish to see in the world – Mahatma Gandhi."

What a quote! But the problem is we can't just change ourselves any more than Moses could make his own face glow. Trying hard is never enough. We are changed by being exposed to the glory of God. We are changed by His Word, by the infilling of the Holy Spirit, and by abiding in Him. I wish I was better at describing this. Really it is freeing, and you don't have to try to produce Godlike qualities in yourself. You just hang out with God, and His nature begins to rub off on you.

In Portland, Oregon, we used to have a mayor who became famous for a photo of himself flashing a painting with the phrase, "Expose Yourself to Art." This may be a crude example, but it is the image I see in my mind. Not baring my body, but my soul, exposing my whole self to the goodness of God. I do this best during worship. Not just singing, mind you, worship. I have to encounter God with my whole heart, in spirit and in truth.

Whenever any believer encounters God in worship, her perspective changes. The more we see Him in His greatness, we see His majesty, His power, and most importantly, we see His love for us. The impossible becomes merely a challenge. We begin to see ourselves differently as well. Instead of mere humans, powerless to change our own circumstances (let alone the world!), we see ourselves as God's own kids, sent on a mission! We're not dependent on our own devices, talents, or gifts; we are fully supported by God to accomplish His purposes. How about you? Are you tired of trying to appear Godly? Would you like to shine like Jesus did? It's not that hard, really. All you have to do is expose yourself to the glory. He does not send us alone. His presence goes with us. He gives us HIS glory!

# FORGIVENESS IS JUST SIMPLE ACCOUNTING

*Forgive us our trespasses as we forgive others*

A s a pastor, helping people forgive seems to be the thing that I do the most. It is just so hard for some people to do. Their hurt is so great. Also, I think that many people really don't know how to forgive or understand what forgiveness is exactly.

I often use my experiences in business to describe the principles to them.

For years, I owned a printing business. My bookkeeper became a believer (at least in my prayers), as payday after payday, one miracle or another would bring in the money needed to meet payroll, sometimes at the very last moment. Needless to say, things were often very tight financially. Living and working in a small town has a lot of challenges, but doing work for someone on credit has to be one of the hardest.

There are only so many businesses in a small town, and within that small pool, I had to compete for their work. I was not the only print shop in town. For every order I received, I had to purchase supplies, pay employees, and of course make my own payments on equipment and overhead. The profit was what I had left over to feed my own family. If one of my customers was having hard times, they might be late paying their bill, which often made me late paying my own bills.

But when months and months went by and a significant customer (with a large bill) didn't pay, things could get serious. After all attempts of collection had failed, I only had one choice: Forgive the debt. I simply removed the sales off my balance sheet as if the bill never happened.

Okay, that's not exactly how you do it. Anyone who has taken simple accounting knows about the T chart of debits and credits. But without trying to teach you the theory of accounting (which I am unqualified to do), suffice it to say everything has to balance. I made it balance by removing the debt.

This T chart, with debits and credits, is like us on the inside. Everything needs to balance. We are all made with a desire for justice and for things to be fair. Whether we are conscious of it or not, we keep a record in our heart. If someone wrongs us, he owes us a debt. We can wait and hope he makes it right by apologizing or something. But all too often he does it again, and his debt to us keeps increasing.

Sometimes a debt is just one occurrence of something so foul we feel we could never forgive.

The problem here is that our lack of forgiveness does nothing to the offender, but it eats away at our own hearts. Unforgiveness can change our personalities from open and trusting to bitter and suspicious of everyone.

Even our bodies respond to unforgiveness. I have seen many people healed of arthritis or stomach disorders after they were able to forgive.

We were not made to carry such resentments.

At the same time, we were created to expect justice. Like the bookkeeper who spends hours trying to find a ten cent discrepancy, we worry over, think about, and strive to make our emotional books balance. It can be difficult for us to find peace if the person who has hurt or offended us does not cooperate in "paying what he owes" in the way we believe he should.

Every Christian knows the Lord's Prayer: *"Forgive us our debts, as we forgive our debtors" (Matthew 6:12, KJV)*. Most know that Jesus said, *"But if you refuse to forgive others, your Father will not forgive your sins" (Matthew 6:14, NLT)*. Emotionally, this just doesn't seem fair. If I am the one who was wronged, why is it that I am being punished for what someone else has done to me?"

God has a different perspective. Consider this story that Jesus told:

*The Parable of the Unmerciful Servant (Matthew 18:21–35, NIV)*

*Then Peter came to Jesus and asked, "Lord, how many times shall I forgive my brother or sister who sins against me? Up to seven times?" Jesus answered, "I tell you, not seven times, but seventy seven times.*

*"Therefore, the kingdom of heaven is like a king who wanted to settle accounts with his servants. As he began the settlement, a man who owed him ten thousand bags of gold was brought to him. Since he was not able to pay, the master ordered that he and his wife and his children and all that he had be sold to repay the debt. At this the servant fell on his knees before him. 'Be patient with me,' he begged, 'and I will pay back everything.' The servant's master took pity on him, canceled the debt and let him go.*

147

*"But when that servant went out, he found one of his fellow ser-*
*vants who owed him a hundred silver coins. He grabbed him and*
*began to choke him. 'Pay back what you owe me!' he demanded. His*
*fellow servant fell to his knees and begged him, 'Be patient with*
*me, and I will pay it back.' But he refused. Instead, he went off and*
*had the man thrown into prison until he could pay the debt. When*
*the other servants saw what had happened, they were outraged and*
*went and told their master everything that had happened. Then*
*the master called the servant in. 'You wicked servant,' he said, 'I*
*canceled all that debt of yours because you begged me to. Shouldn't*
*you have had mercy on your fellow servant just as I had on you?' In*
*anger his master handed him over to the jailers to be tortured, until*
*he should pay back all he owed. This is how my heavenly Father will*
*treat each of you unless you forgive your brother or sister from your*
*heart."*

"Wow! That's harsh," you say?

Let's look at that T chart again. Only now, what happens if we put on there the realistic debt that we owe? The Bible says, *"For the wages of sin is death ..." (Romans 6:23, NIV).*

Let that reality sink in.

We could never pay that debt, no matter how good we try to be.

Now, let the grace of the Lord sink in. You and I as Christians don't have to pay the price of the debt we owe. He doesn't even want us to run around feeling guilty! We should be full of joy that our debt has been paid in full.

I remember a chorus we used to sing:

*He paid a debt He did not owe,*

*I owed a debt I could not pay,*

*I needed someone to wash my sins away.*

*And now I sing a brand new song,*

*"Amazing Grace."*

*Christ Jesus paid a debt that I could never pay.*

Oh, but there is one condition, we have to forgive others.

## Forgiveness and Trust

When you fully realize that the grace the Lord has given you more than covers what others may owe you, you will be able to forgive easily!

"What?!?!?" you say. "What if they do it again? What do I do then?" "Seventy seven times" or "Seventy times seven" is what Jesus said. Sometimes that is hard to wrap our minds around. However in my business, I found a simple solution.

People think that businesses need "write offs." Some of them seem to think that when a business writes something off, it somehow saves them money. This is not entirely true. When the man did not pay his printing bill (money that I badly needed), I eventually wrote the bill off on my taxes. What that really meant was that after spending all the money on the materials and payroll to produce his project, I gave up expecting him to pay and now chose not to pay taxes on the money I never received. This was really hard for me to do at the time. I knew the guy was going through hard times, but so was I! Even more so because of his decisions! I finally forgave the debt. As a Christian, I knew I had to forgive him.

You would think that this would be the end of the story, but no! About a year later the same man came into my print shop as if nothing had ever happened, wanting to order printing…and he wanted it on credit!

Now my first inclination was to tell him, "When you pay your old bill, we can talk about it." But the Lord reminded me that he no longer owed that bill, I had written it off! As my peace was being challenged internally, I realized the correct and just solution. He no longer owed the bill, and as such I had no legitimate reason not to do more printing for him. (I also really needed more work!) But doing printing for him didn't mean that I had to extend credit to him. In fact, I required a deposit before I started!

I began to explain to him my decision. I told him that he would have to earn back my trust before I extended credit to him again. In time, we would reconsider if things could go back to the way they were before his bankruptcy. In time they did and he became one of my best customers, who faithfully paid his bills.

This principle is also true in our personal relationships. Just because we have forgiven someone does not mean that they automatically earn back our trust. They no longer owe us for past deeds. That is all. Many people confuse this part and refuse to forgive because they think that if they forgive, they will have to act as if nothing ever happened. This is not true.

### Trust is earned.

You would not lend your car to a stranger off the street. Nor would you lend your car to someone you previously trusted who returned it with beer bottles inside. It is the same way after you forgive people. They now deserve the same grace as anyone else, but they will have to earn your trust by acting trustworthy in relationship with you, just like anyone else would.

## *Forgiveness Is a Decision*

Another thing about forgiveness, "excusing a debt" is not the same as "forgiving" one.

For instance, let's say you have a hard time believing that you can be smart. In trying to figure out why, a memory surfaces of your mother calling you stupid when you were young. In this sort of situation, it can be easy to say to yourself or even in prayer: "My mom called me 'stupid,' but I know she didn't really mean it…" or "Mom called me 'stupid,' but I know she only said that because…." Excusing her behavior might make you feel better in the moment, but it won't result in healing. You will still suffer from the results of the "word curse" over your life.

But think about it, if Jesus already paid the whole price for your mother's sin against you, why minimize it? Instead, call it what it is: a sin, a debt owed to you, a crime that no mother should ever commit against her child. And then forgive it. That's what forgiveness is: a decision, a simple act of accounting. We say out loud what actually happened, acknowledge how truly wrong it really was, and choose to forgive what the other person owes us. Because Jesus forgave you, your mother no longer owes anything. Now you can look at that curse and confidently know that it was wrong, it was not the truth. You've covered over those words with the love and forgiveness and grace of Jesus. They no longer have any power. You were created in God's image and therefore can be absolutely brilliant!

Do not be afraid of calling sin "sin" when forgiving. Doing so might bring up painful feelings of resentment inside of you. That's okay! Let them out. It is those very feelings that you are trying to get rid of. Don't stuff them now!

Finally, I want to address the "feelings of forgiveness." Many people have tried to forgive but have concluded that they must not have forgiven because the feelings remained. They didn't feel any different, so they must not have truly forgiven. This is not necessarily true.

Feelings are funny (strange). We often use our feelings to determine what is true and what is false. But our feelings can lie.

Suppose I lied to you and told you one of your loved ones was killed in an auto accident. If you trusted me, you would immediately feel overwhelming grief and sadness. Your feelings would respond to what you believed to be true. But if the whole thing was based on a lie, then all of the feelings of grief were for nothing.

In the same way, when we forgive we may not immediately feel better. Our faith is not based on how we feel but in the contract that we have just made with God. I call it "doing the paperwork." (Side note: God can't and won't forgive for you. You have to do your own paperwork. Praying "Dear God, please help me to forgive ____" isn't actually forgiveness. Forgiveness is when we say, "Dear God, I choose to forgive ____.") Whenever I lead someone through a prayer of forgiveness, I ask the Holy Spirit to remind them when they are later tempted to take back their decision.

I say when, not if. When we forgive, we will be tempted to take up the offense again. The enemy of our souls knows the power of unforgiveness to separate us from the grace of God. He wants you to take it back. He wants you to be bitter and hurt. But when the temptation comes, we simply remind ourselves, the devil, and all of heaven, "That debt has been paid." We repeat this as many times as necessary. Before long, our feelings will agree.

## *Forgiveness Sets Us Free*

When we forgive, we are choosing to allow the grace of God (who forgave us and paid our own debt) to also cover the debt of the person who has offended us. When I think about it that way, it IS easy! Between the God who loves me and the person who offended me, who is more trustworthy to cover the debt owed? God, of course!

When we choose not to forgive, or avoid it simply because of the pain involved, we remain in bondage; but when we choose to forgive, those chains are released. The peace and joy and even love that fills our heart replace the torment that we were struggling with. No one was wronged more than Jesus. And no one deserved it less. I think of the verse where Jesus said,

> *"In this world you will have trouble, but take heart, I have overcome the world" (John 16:33, NIV).*

We consider Jesus to be the most powerful man to have ever lived. Forgiveness is not weak. It is strength personified in Jesus. You hold that power yourself when you forgive.

# EATING THE FRUIT OF LIES

*You are what you eat*

There is a saying, "You are what you eat." It is normally associated with a food diet and health, but the same is true about spiritual health.

In Proverbs it says,

*"For as he thinketh in his heart, so is he" (Proverbs 23:7, KJV).*

As a father, I have three daughters and a son. Like most dads, I like to fix things, especially for my children. When my daughters became teenagers, each of them had a day when they came home crying, believing that they were ugly. This, of course, was not true, but there was nothing I could say at the time to convince them otherwise. Something had happened. Someone had said something, and somehow they believed a lie. Once the lie took root, the truth seemed like a fantasy. My encouragement to them that they were beautiful, while appreciated, was quickly brushed aside as flattery.

Each of us battle in our thought life with the enemy of our souls. Most of these battles center around our identity. I, for instance, am either the biggest impostor on the face of the earth (which is what I hear from the enemy constantly when I am filled with doubt), or I am who God says I am. (I am too embarrassed to even mention what I think He says about me.) Unfortunately, there are days when there is much more evidence that I am an impostor than that I am someone of importance with something to offer. Sometimes I get discouraged and think to myself, "Just who do you think you are?" and I want to quit. It's easy to believe the lies.

No one sets out to believe a lie. We probably wouldn't believe them if there wasn't so much compelling evidence to support them! Sadly, there is often convincing evidence. Our past failures, the judgments of others, and even our own feelings seem to scream at us that we are disqualified from reaching the hope of His calling. The devil will even try to use Scripture to deceive us, like he did Jesus in the wilderness (see Matthew 4:1–11).

I've found that one of the most common phrases he (the devil) uses with me is "just be realistic." It seems that to be realistic is to judge my current situation based on the laws of nature and past experience alone. When I do that, God's promises become wishful thinking and the stuff of fantasy. I begin to doubt, just like Adam and Eve in the Garden of Eden, when the snake said, *"...Did God really say...?"* (Genesis 3:1, NIV).

Oh, it gets worse! The enemy doesn't stop at discouragement. He wants to utterly destroy us and to stop us from ever making any impact in the world. So now, once we doubt what God has said on one thing, he quickly shifts to use that as "evidence" in his crusade to cause us to wonder about everything that God has said. If we're not careful, it doesn't take long to find ourselves rendered impotent, depressed, and wondering why God has abandoned us (another lie). This is what I call eating the fruit of lies.

Consider this verse:

> *"You have plowed iniquity; you have reaped injustice; you have eaten the fruit of lies. Because you have trusted in your own way"* *(Hosea 10:13, ESV).*

Isn't that just like a prophet? When you are already down and depressed, he comes and rebukes you! You would think that a loving, compassionate God would come, pat your head, and soothingly say, "You poor baby." But He can't; He can't agree with the lie that you believe.

### *Where Do You Get Your Truth?*

We are told to *"meditate on the Word" (Psalm 119:148, NIV).* Consider the shepherd boy, David, in the Bible. He meditated on God's Word day and night; he ate the fruit of the Truth. When David appeared on the battlefield where Goliath was threatening the armies of God, he was the only one who was able to see a reality where Goliath could be beaten. Others were being "realistic." Probably most of the other soldiers were willing to die for their family and friends, but they could not realistically claim that they could defeat the nine foot tall warrior.

They were insulted that David believed that he could! This is a case where the lie made more sense than the truth. But David had been eating from a different reality. From David's point of view, any man, even one who was nine feet tall, was no match for the Living God. David wasn't trusting in his own strength but in the unlimited power of God. In his mind, God was real, His Word was true, not just fantasy or wishful thinking, and His promises were as good as gold. David was so sure of God's backing that he even asked, *"...What will be done for the man who kills this Philistine?..." (1 Samuel 17:26, NIV)* For David, this was like betting on a sure thing.

Think about it! David was so confident that he was able to convince King Saul to let him fight, even though he was not even big enough to wear Saul's armor. I am sure that at least some of the soldiers had second thoughts over this deal. Sizing him up, a few of them had to think, "I could take that kid easy! Goliath is going to eat him for lunch, and we will all be slaves as a result."

The other soldiers in the army believed a lie that the man who faced Goliath would face him alone, that he was limited to his own abilities.

In the same way, we too often look to our own talents or resources when we face challenges. When our own resources aren't enough, we despair because we can "do the math" and predict the future. The "facts" seem truer than the promises of God. The enemy will harass us with all sorts of reasons why we need to be realistic instead of trusting in God's promises. What is worse is when we create a lifestyle of living realistically that causes us to ignore the vast resources of heaven that are available to us.

Sadly, most of us never enter into the reality of what is available to those who believe.

In the book of Revelation, there is a verse that just astounds me:

> *"But outside are dogs and sorcerers and sexually immoral and murderers and idolaters, and whoever loves and practices a lie" (Revelations 22:15, NKJV).*

Being deceived into believing a lie has the same effect as sin, it cuts us off from experiencing the goodness of God. Most of us can understand that murderers would not enter into God's blessings. Many people don't realize that believing a lie also keeps us from experiencing what God has for us.

## Jesus, Don't You Care?

Even Jesus' disciples fell into the trap of believing lies when they were scared. They went so far as to question whether or not He cared if they lived or died in the boat with Jesus during a storm (see Mark 4:35–41)! Now, I like to fish and many times I have been out to sea when the water was rough. On a few occasions, things looked really bad to me, as the big boat I was on dipped so low in the swells of the ocean that you could rarely even see the horizon. But one thing calmed me: the captain showed no sign of being afraid. He had obviously seen worse and wasn't worried.

In Jesus' case, the professional fishermen were afraid. When they woke Jesus up they cried, *"Don't You care that we are about to die?" (Mark 4:38, my paraphrase)* The facts were clear to them. They were the experts; they knew all about sea travel and storms. They believed a lie, and they didn't even know it! They forgot Who was in the boat. Oh, they knew Jesus was there, they just forgot who He was. You can tell this by the first part of their question *"Don't You care?"*

Accusing God of not caring seems to be one of the most obvious symptoms of believing a lie. In dark times, two of the first lies the enemy throws out to see if we'll bite on them are: "God doesn't really love you" and "God has abandoned you." They're lies, of course. And yet, when we are tricked, when we have been deceived, it seems to us that all the facts prove that the lie is in fact the truth. We can become so convinced of a lie in our own minds that the truth feels like a lie to us. The disciples swallowed lies hook, line, and sinker (pun intended). They forgot who Jesus was. In spite of all the miracles they had seen, when the sea was calm and the wind ceased, they asked each other, *"Who is this? Even the wind and the waves obey him!"* (Mark 4:41, NIV).

## Has God Really Said?

Maybe it is oversimplifying things, but it seems to me that most of these lies come down to the challenge, "Who do you think you are?" The enemy will challenge the character of God, God's promises, and our own right to believe that these promises belong to us.

To quote the devil, "Has God really said…?"

- You are more than conquerors, through Christ Jesus (Romans 8:37).
- You are kings and priests (Revelation 1:6).
- You are ambassadors from heaven to earth (2 Corinthians 5:20).
- You are sent by God to be an example (witness) (Acts 1:8).
- You are children of the Father, and He loves you (1 John 3:1).
- You are friends of the Lord Jesus Christ (John 15:13–15).
- You are filled with the Holy Spirit of God. (1 John 2:20).
- You can do all things through Christ (Philippians 4:13).
- God shall provide all your needs (Philippians 4:19).

Even as I am writing this, I hear a voice in my head saying, "But Raaaaaandyyyy, these are just Bible stories; I have real problems, I am not some Bible character." Maybe that's what you're thinking. Okay, I will give you that for a moment. Maybe you are not one of the disciples or King David, but has God changed? Did He love them more than you?

Maybe you aren't going to war against a nine foot tall giant. Maybe your giant is a big bill, or hopelessness over ever finding a mate, or having a child. Maybe you are dealing with sickness. Your giant could be any number of other things.

I have seen these and many other kinds of giants fall. I have watched them fall for ordinary people, not just for superstars or Bible characters. But the rules are the same. God is the same.

I believe that God was determined to defeat Goliath and deliver Israel from the Philistines, but the soldiers on the battlefield with Saul couldn't see it because they had believed a lie. The difference between David and every other soldier on the field wasn't strength or skill. The difference was that David believed God.

Many have gone without, not because God did not care, but because they believed a lie that somehow these blessings were not for them.

## *A Promise Fulfilled*

I understand this because I've been in the same place where God's promises felt like a cruel joke. It took everything in me not to believe the lie.

Many years ago, my dream of becoming a pastor came true. I sold my printing business and lived on the proceeds just for the opportunity. I had an amazing time with more miracles and people coming to Christ than I could have ever imagined. But after a year, the money dried up, the church began to have many problems (I was an assistant pastor), and eventually it closed.

Poor and disillusioned, I got a job and began a very slow and difficult journey of rebuilding my life. I felt that God had let me down. Or worse, that I had let Him down and that I just wasn't good enough. People who used to treat me with respect (either as a business owner or as a pastor) now seemed to avoid me. I used to be someone; now I felt like a nobody and a failure.

I had a hard time even going to church. How could I go back to just attending after all I had experienced? Year after year went by in the greatest desert of my life. Eventually I bought another printing business and poured myself into my business, working fourteen hours a day, six and seven days a week. But I was dead inside with my dream totally destroyed.

In spite of my struggles, the depth of my relationship with God prevailed. Even though I was still disillusioned, I could never go back to the world. I had found the truth; there was nowhere else to go.

> *"After the crowds left Him, Jesus asked His disciples, 'Do you also want to go away?' But Simon Peter answered Him, 'Lord, to whom shall we go? You have the words of eternal life'"* (John 6:67–68, NKJV).

I felt the same way.

This was my spiritual condition one day in my printing business office while witnessing to an alcoholic employee that there was still hope for Him in Jesus. Somehow in the course of the conversation, I heard myself say, "I know that I will be a pastor again someday because that is the call on my life." Immediately, I was overwhelmed with a sense as if I had just told a lie. I could think of no possible way that what I had just said would ever come to pass.

Sure, I believed that God had called me to be a pastor, but maybe He just meant for that one year. Heck, I didn't even go to church at that time; I wasn't even sure what I believed about church anymore! How was I ever going to be a pastor again? After a great deal of inner struggle, I went to prayer and gave it all back to God. I chose to believe what I thought God was saying. The whole idea seemed impossible, but if God still wanted me, I was still available. He would have to do it because I had no idea how it could ever happen. Then I completely forgot about it.

To make a very long story short, after a number of years, I was a pastor again. God asked me to start Solomon's Porch.

One day, a pastor friend of mine asked me to go with him to a pastors' meeting in Tigard. I was so honored to be asked that I even agreed to go after he said that something had come up and he couldn't attend, but he really wanted me to go anyway. He gave me the address and even though it looked familiar, I didn't give it a second thought until I arrived at the church office where we were supposed to meet.

I looked around and realized I was sitting in the very same room that used to be my own office at the printing company. The room where I declared, even though it felt like a lie, that God was still able to fulfill my destiny. Only now I stood in the very same place as a pastor. Later, I testified to the other pastors of the miracle that had just happened.

No matter how many times I tell that story, it never seems to have the impact on others that I feel myself. It takes my breath away. Even typing it right now, it brings me to tears because to me it felt totally impossible. It was beyond a pipe dream. It made me feel sad just to think about it. And yet, God is faithful. He never forgot, He never stopped caring, and my life IS important to Him.

Which version of the truth are you believing today?

# IT'S OK TO BE ME

*"For you formed my inward parts; You covered me in my mother's womb. I will praise You, for I am fearfully and wonderfully made" (Psalm 139:13-14a, NKJV).*

Everyone has a need for significance. We all want to matter. In my generation, many of us got saved through the tract, *The Four Spiritual Laws*, which declared, "God loves you and has a wonderful plan for your life." While true, finding that plan, that destiny, can be a puzzle that stumps a lot of people.

Comparison hides at the heart of the problem. We compare our lives and experiences to the superstars of TV, movies, or the stories we read in books. Many a girl has been utterly despondent because she compared her looks to some airbrushed and starved model in a magazine ad, feeling unable to measure up.

I did even worse. I compared my life and experiences to the superstars of the pulpit. I loved the traveling evangelists who would come to our church once a year. Their stories of adventures, the miracles that happened through their ministries, and the many people who got saved made me think that God must really love them. I wanted to be just like that. I wanted (and still do) to be as effective as I could be for the Lord.

But as hard as I tried, I just couldn't reproduce the same results as the stories I had heard. I felt so disheartened! I wondered if God simply loved them more than me. It seemed as if certain people in the world were "special," and I wasn't one of them. That didn't sit well with me. The Bible says that, "…*God is no respecter of persons*" *(Acts 10:34, KJV )*. I took that to mean: What He will do for one, He will do for all. Why couldn't I break through and become one of the special ones?

This may seem like an absurd topic to you, but it has taken most of my life to learn what should be most basic for all of us: It is okay to be me. No, it is not just okay, but great, or as Tony the Tiger says, "Grr-reat!"

There is nobody that I would rather be than the person who God created me to be. I am the only one like me, an original! As hard as you try, you can't be me as well as I can be me. I know this sounds silly, but bear with me a bit longer.

You see, from a worldly point of view, in order to be great, you have to be better than someone else at something. Even Jesus' own disciples argued over who was the greatest (see Luke 9:46). Why? Because they all wanted to be loved and significant. And obviously, whoever is the best is loved the most. Right??? Who makes it their goal to be second best, let alone last?

But God is not running a contest. He is a father who is more than able to love all of His children immensely, appreciating the little nuances of each of His kids. I know; you probably think you already understand, but please bear with me a little more.

You see, when I first became a father I was really afraid that I wouldn't love my child enough. What I found out was that I loved my daughter more than life itself. I couldn't explain it, but it was true. Then my wife became pregnant with our second, and I was really worried. Oh, how unfair it would be to this second child. I could never love anyone as much as I loved my firstborn. How was I going to divide my love between them? Really silly, right?

Well, I found out what every parent already knows. You don't have to divide what love you have between your children, your love multiplies. I love each of my children more than life itself.

## *God Loves Who You Are Today*

I have a friend who worked very hard at everything. It seemed that no matter what she did, an inner voice kept telling her she could do better. The hours she spent in prayer and intercession, Bible study, service to others and the church felt to her like they were never enough. She appraised her appearance and everything else according to what others thought. After years of encouraging her that God was proud of her, and that being herself was not only "good enough" but it was the very best, she finally got it. She came by one day just to report, *"It's okay to be me!"*

How free and full of joy she was! God loved her. Not some perfect image of who she could be, but who she was today.

The peace of letting go of comparisons and worries about what others think, knowing that who you are is exactly who you are supposed to be, is one of the most powerful experiences a Christian can have. Some people wonder if believing "It's okay to be me" changes the motivation people feel to serve, study, or grow. Well, it changes it, yes, but it does not take the motivation away. In this new way of living, your goal becomes simply to be the best you that you can be. It is a goal that you can accomplish, knowing that succeed or fail, your heavenly Father is proud of you no matter what. He is on your side, cheering for you, not waiting until someday when you finally figure it all out.

A person who is comfortable in her own skin is powerful. She no longer is a slave to what others may think or to how they judge her. People like this are free to risk believing God because failure is only another step toward success. Earthly parents do not punish a child for falling while trying to learn to walk or ride a bike. Why would we think that God would be unhappy with us as we learn to walk by faith?

## God's Economy

The economy of God is much different than the way we perceive things. The person born into a wealthy family, who receives an expensive education, has more opportunity than someone who does not have these things. Even gifted people have received "gifts." In other words, they did not earn them. The Bible tells us that, "*...From everyone who has been given much, much will be required...*" *(Luke 12:48)*. So why is it that we compare ourselves to others?

What may be an incredible struggle for one person may just come naturally for another. We each have our own life to walk out. We can save so much time and discouragement by working with what God has given us, both gifts and challenges, instead of trying to compare and live up to other people's expectations.

In the parable of the talents, what do you think would have resulted if the servant given ten talents was the one who buried them? And how would the master have responded to the faithful servant, even if he received only one talent at the start? The faithful servant, no matter how much he received, would have been given even more in the end. God is not more pleased with those He has given the most to; He is most pleased with those who do the most they can with what they have been given.

I did not grow up in a wealthy family. In fact, with my father being an alcoholic, I grew up mostly on welfare, living in a low income housing project in the inner city. Drugs, crime, and one parent families were the norm, and no one ever seemed to get out. Advanced education was not an option; in fact, I only finished high school with a GED. I didn't even think I would live to be twenty one.

Then I got saved. Jesus changed everything in my life. He gave me a hope and a future.

## Walking Into a Calling Takes Time

At the same time, I got married to my wonderful wife, Jodene. From the very beginning, I heard a call to ministry; but it seemed that I just wasn't good enough to be in ministry. Even if I were to receive a scholarship to go to Bible school, I wouldn't be able to go because I had a family to support and limited resources. I was only qualified to get a minimum wage job, and now I had the responsibilities of a family to support. Still I responded to every altar call for those willing to "stand in the gap," to do the work of the Lord.

This rousing message that I heard wherever I went would thrill and inspire the congregations, but to me it became a source of great sadness. I would run (yes, run) up front. In one case at a Corrie Ten Boom event, I literally stood on my seat and shouted the prayer response, only to find that I was the only one standing and praying aloud, with everyone looking at me. At this point my wife was trying to hide under her seat in embarrassment. It seemed to me that while God was "looking for a man," I was waving my hand shouting, "Pick me, pick me" only to have God declare that He was still looking for someone, anyone, but me.

One day another evangelist came to our church and preached virtually the same message again. When the altar call came I remained in my seat, too discouraged to respond even though there was nothing I wanted more. He kept on calling. He knew that someone was supposed to respond who hadn't yet. Finally I rose slowly, and immediately He stopped what he was doing and prophesied over me about my life and my ministry. His words were exactly what have happened in the last forty years. Of course, at the time, I thought it would all begin immediately. It didn't.

Around the same time, I encountered another prophet from God who spoke into my life. At the time, I was trying to make a living in my father's print shop. Daily I would go door to door to businesses, trying to sell printing. I gave out hundreds of business cards, working from early morning till late at night. Little did I realize that I was a poorly dressed kid (20 years old) trying to compete with professional salesmen who represented businesses worth millions of dollars. All of the equipment we owned in the print shop in the basement of my father's home would be worth just a few hundred dollars.

As a member of Full Gospel Business Men's Fellowship International, every Tuesday I attended a luncheon with a room full of mostly successful businessmen. There were doctors, lawyers, politicians, pro athletes and many business owners. I don't know if I ever sold any printing there, but I enjoyed the testimonies and friendships I made with other Christian businessmen who had a passion for reaching people for Jesus.

One day a special speaker came to town. He had an amazing testimony about how God had called him to raise 20 million dollars to build a church in Ireland. He talked about how he was basically a nobody (like me), not even the most gifted or talented in his coal miner family, and yet God called him to do it. He had no money of his own, but he felt led to announce that God would give him the money in one offering at the local coliseum on a specific date. Even though religious broadcasting was illegal in Ireland at the time, the media broadcast his whole message widely as news of the event. After sharing the Gospel, he took the offering and received all the money God had promised.

For me, the real miracle is what happened next in that lunch meeting. This speaker (I don't remember his name) declared, "I have come to the U.S. and have shared my testimony all around this country, but I was sent here to deliver a message from God to one man." I was that man. Truly the very least of anyone in that room that day. And the message? It was from Scripture:

> I returned, and saw under the sun, that the race is not to the swift, nor the battle to the strong, neither yet bread to the wise, nor yet riches to men of understanding, nor yet favor to men of skill; but time and chance happeneth to them all (Ecclesiastes 9:11, KJV).

That was almost 40 years ago, and even still that verse is precious to me. It means that God is with me. I am not limited to my own talents or abilities. He is all I need.

For thirty years I dreamed of going to the mission field. Over the years, I had many invitations to go to many countries. But I couldn't afford to go. I beat myself up thinking, "If only I had more faith, God would give me the money to go." Years of barely supporting my family and struggling businesses made it seem as if my time would never come.

Well, a lot happened during those years, and eventually I became pastor of a church with more ministry opportunities than I had energy to accomplish. One day an invitation came again. Yes, I still wanted to go, but... I still didn't have the money for travel, and my health wasn't the best (I've had three heart attacks). A friend promised that she would take the responsibility of raising the funds if I would just say yes. Later when my wife was really concerned regarding my health, the same friend (a nurse) quit her job and traveled with me so that my wife would not have to worry so much.

After all the years of wishing to be part of a ministry team that went overseas just to serve, I was the keynote speaker wherever I went! I spoke up to seven times a day, ministering in village churches, hospitals, orphanages, schools, and even on the radio to millions of listeners. I saw lots of people receive Christ as their Savior and receive miraculous healings and deliverances. I got to be an encouragement to many pastors of small village churches. My dream had been fulfilled beyond my wildest imagining.

Today, I continue to go back to Africa. When I go, I do not put on big crusades or start great ministries. I go to the smallest village churches and to the least of the street children and orphans. I encourage them that God thinks they are important and significant. To God, every one of them is his favorite.

God did not make a mistake when he made you. Whether rich or poor, regardless of race or gender, God carefully formed you with a wonderful destiny in mind. He compares you to no other, and He watches with anticipation as you walk through the challenges and adventures that He has set before you.

# WHY AM I SHAKING?

## Godly Encounters

I have had just a few experiences that literally changed my life. But it doesn't take very many. For me, most of these encounters with God have been accompanied with physical manifestations (such as crying, shaking, falling down, or laughing) in response to the presence of God that may appear strange to others. I tell these stories to people when they are skeptical about whether God is actually involved in the physical manifestations that sometimes come with an encounter with God.

As an onlooker, it can be easy to judge these kinds of things as emotionalism, deception from the enemy, or showmanship. I had doubts at first myself. It's easy to be critical of some of the mysterious manifestations that happen when God touches someone. And frankly, like anything authentic, there are counterfeits. I have been in meetings where preachers literally pushed people down and called it God. So, I understand why people are skeptical, but when it is a real touch from God, it can be life changing.

## *I Never Knew*

Years ago, I had a man come to one of my meetings. I recognized him because I had performed his daughter's wedding and had gotten to know him a little during that time. I knew him well enough to know that mine was not his kind of meeting. He was an elder in his church and had been a faithful Christian for many, many years, but supernatural things were not, shall we say, part of his comfort zone.

This particular meeting was one of those special meetings where God showed up in power. People were healed and touched by God in many miraculous ways. Many had been "slain in the Spirt". He came up to me for prayer and said, "I am not going to fall down." I smiled and told him that I didn't need him to fall down for my ego, but asked him to be open to whatever God had for him. He said that this was what he wanted: more of God and whatever God had for him.

I sensed what was going to happen, so I took a couple of steps back (about 10 feet away) and asked the Holy Spirit to fall on him. He was instantly slain in the Spirit. The presence of God was so strong on him that he fell to the floor and could not get up for over an hour. God was speaking to him and loving on him. When he could finally speak, through tears and awe, he pulled my face to his and said, "I never knew. I never knew that God could be so real!" This precious man, who had served God faithfully for so many years encountered the tangible presence and love of God for the first time, his life was changed that night.

Another time a young lady came up in the prayer line during one of my meetings. I did not know her; it was her first time to our church. I also didn't know that she was convinced that any kind of physical manifestation was fake or emotionalism. I was just praying for people. She had sworn to herself that, "If he pushes me over I am going to get right back up and give him a piece of my mind." When I went to pray for her I got that same feeling that I should stand back, and sure enough she went down. In fact, I heard many years later that she actually felt a hand on her forehead push her over. But, when she looked up and saw where I was, she knew it was not my hand but God's. Her life was changed that day. She knew for herself that God is real and still does things today. Many years later she gave all her savings to support an orphanage in Africa.

## Signs and Wonders

In the early eighties, I went to a conference in Anaheim, California called "Signs and Wonders and Church Growth." John Wimber was the main speaker. Prior to this experience, about the only manifestations I had seen were people crying or being slain in the Spirit. Both were controversial at the time, and many judged these things, saying that they were not from God. I had not seen many manifestations of the Holy Spirit, but I had read about them throughout church history. In fact, I wanted to believe that God still did things like that, but I in no way understood them.

At the conference, I saw things I had never seen before. Worship was amazing! I literally saw the Holy Spirit moving among the people. You couldn't see Him, but it looked like He was moving His hand like wind on a wheat field. I heard stories of amazing healings and how miracles were bringing thousands to Christ. It was what John called, "Doing the stuff."

During one of the morning sessions, John got up to the microphone. Now, I had never seen anyone like him. Here he was, a very important speaker on stage, in front of 5000 pastors and leaders, and he was dressed in a Hawaiian shirt and shorts! I was used to the suit and tie kind of preachers. He stood up and said, "God wants to do something. Come Holy Spirit."

We waited for what seemed like forever, but it was probably only five minutes (still a long time for silence in a meeting). John just stood there smiling. No urging, no rousing speech; he just stood there smiling. When nothing seemed to be happening, he just shrugged his shoulders, kept smiling, and waiting.

Eventually, I heard a loud cry way across the room. Honestly, my only thought was, "There is one in every crowd." I just thought someone was trying to make something happen. Then I noticed that more and more people around her were also crying, and it was growing. I looked up to John hoping that he would say something to get things under control, but he just stood there, smiling. It got worse as more and more people started crying, wailing, as if they were women in labor pains. It was growing... becoming like a wave, and it was coming my way! I vowed right there that even if I was the only person in the whole place still standing and not crying, I was not going to fake it. Before I knew what hit me, I was on my face, crying out to God to restore the church to be the example to the world that He originally intended.

It kept coming in waves; the intensity of the intercession inside of me would increase and decrease in waves, as the hand of God moved over the congregation.

Finally John spoke. He said, "Ok, let it go now. That was just God showing you His heart for the church."

Well, THAT got my attention.

As the conference went on, John and others taught the Word like I had never heard before. They shared story after story of how the miracles of God were part of every move of the Spirit; every revival throughout history. How signs and wonders were God's tools for evangelism. I had come to the same conclusion, but I'd never actually seen it happen. Not like this! After each meeting I saw people being healed and others getting touched by God. But, instead of just falling down, many of these people began to shake.

## Shaking

At an afternoon workshop, Blaine Cook (John's assistant pastor at that time), taught on the parable of the sower. He told amazing stories of how he had seen hundreds come to Christ and of all the miracles he had seen. At the end he gave an altar call for any who wanted more, who were willing to take divine appointments from God, and share the gospel in power.

I was one of maybe 300 people who went forward. As Blaine prayed, my right hand started to shake. I told myself that it was just me, wanting it too bad or something. I put my hand in my pocket. Then my left hand started to shake, and I did the same thing. Then my right leg, so I pushed it down, but when I did that my left leg did the same. This was really strange; I didn't know what was happening. I must have been quite a sight, because Blaine called out to me and said, "That is God. Why don't you just let Him touch you?"

So I took my hands out of my pockets, and before long I was shaking from head to toe. This went on for a long time, especially when people would come by to pray for me. They would just hold out their hands and pray, "More Lord." Whenever they said this, the shaking would increase. Then, someone came and rebuked me, saying I was faking it, and it slowed. I knew I wasn't faking it, but I didn't understand what was happening. I wondered if it was just some involuntary reaction to wanting to be touched by God so bad.

It was time to go to dinner (they were turning out the lights and clearing the hall), but I was still shaking. It had been over an hour. My friends guided me through the church to the car. When we got to the restaurant, I was still trembling and told them I would be in in a bit. Sitting in the back seat of the car, I prayed, "God, I can't go in there like this." It started to ease, but then I prayed, "But God, I can't go home the same," and I shook so hard I bumped my head on the roof of the car. After a few minutes…the shaking eased to just trembling so I decided to go in.

As I got to the crosswalk, I stood next to someone selling flowers. I thought I heard the Lord tell me to talk to her about Him. I quickly blew it off as my imagination and went into the restaurant. I went to the table and ordered. My friends were making fun of me nicely. I couldn't hold a fork.

I went to call my wife who was back at home. As I talked with her, I could overhear the person in the booth next to me (remember this was 1984, before cell phones); this person was talking really crude sex talk and then I thought I heard the Lord tell me to tell him about real love. Again, I blew this off as just me. I finished my call and went back to my dinner. I picked up my fork and began to eat. It was then I realized that I wasn't shaking anymore. I quickly remembered the two opportunities that I had to witness that I had passed up.

I tell you this without exaggeration. I got up from the table and ran to the bathroom where I got down on my knees and cried and prayed, "Please don't give up on me Lord." Eventually, I got up sadly and went and ate. No more shaking…I didn't hear anything.

We went back for the evening session. It was another wonderful meeting with many people receiving healing. Afterwards, I noticed Blaine talking and praying for people. I was used to the important people leaving soon after the meetings, not mingling, and talking to attendees. But here he was, so up I went. After waiting my turn, I asked him, "Nice trick, why was I shaking?" He said he didn't know. I said, "You don't understand. I don't believe in shaking." He said, "It must be the Holy Spirit." I said, "I am an elder in a Pentecostal church, President of a Full Gospel Businessman's chapter, and I have never seen this before."

Blaine kindly just said, "Here, let me pray for you again." He prayed in that strange Vineyard way... all casual with his eyes open. He said, "Come Holy Spirit." Sure enough, I began to shake. In fact, I shook so hard that I began to bounce on my heels. I bounced backwards about 100 feet, and he called me back again. He prayed again and the same thing happened.

Blaine called me back one more time. This time he asked me, "Do you believe in mantles of anointing?" I said, "I think so." He said, "Did you know that John believes that he has the same mantle that was on George Fox (the founder of the Quakers)?" "Yes, I had heard that," I answered. He said, "John prayed for me to carry that same anointing, and sometimes God directs me to give it away to others. Would you like that?" I replied, "Yes."

Everything I had seen, the intercession, the healings, the shaking, the hand of God, these were amazing, but what Blaine Cook prayed, changed my life. He prayed, "God, I esteem Randy as better than myself, and I ask that all You have given to me that You would give to him." I was speechless. I just graciously thanked him and walked away. Esteemed ME better than himself? How could that be? He was a well known speaker with many powerful testimonies.

I chose to believe that I had received something from God; that I was going home changed, and I would look for divine appointments to share the gospel. I had to drive all night and most of the next day to get home. After I got home I received a phone call from my pastor, "Where are you?" he said. "I just got home. I haven't even showered and church is already started. I just thought I'd see you next week," I replied. "No," he said, "you are speaking tonight about your trip."

I just went as I was and got to church just as worship was ending. I was not much of a public speaker, so I just shared the testimonies about what had happened.

While I was speaking, the Holy Spirit fell on our church. It was chaos like a bomb had gone off. Some people were standing with their arms up to heaven praising God. Others were on their knees crying. Some were… well, they were shaking just like I had been. They had never seen anything like it before. We were a church that believed in healing and moves of the Spirit, but rarely saw either. Now, here we were. I don't know how many people were healed that night, but it was a lot, and everybody was touched by God.

The next day the pastor came to my business and, in tears, confessed that he had prayed for years for what had happened the night before. We prayed thanking God; both of us in tears and so grateful.

## Divine Appointments

As I said, my life was changed. I had a new prayer, "Lord, if you have a divine appointment for me today, I am available." I would pray this prayer every day. Every day I would get a divine appointment of some kind. I literally had people come up to me and ask how to be saved. I already shared the KFC story, but stories like that happened every day.

One day, I almost forgot to pray my prayer. I had sold my print shop and become an assistant pastor at my church. I had been teaching 12 times a week, as well as counseling and performing other pastoral duties while my pastor was gone for over a month. When Graham got back, he sent my wife and I to the beach to get a break. It was a great idea, and we had a wonderful day. Unfortunately, there were no vacancies in the motels. We decided to just go to a movie and go home.

As I was driving back to Salem with my wife asleep, it hit me that I'd forgotten to pray my prayer. "Oh, no! I don't want to take a vacation from YOU Lord. If You have a divine appointment for me tonight, I am available." It was already late, but we went to the last showing of the evening at the theater.

The movie seemed out of focus to me. As a printer, sharp images are a kind of a fetish. I commented to my wife about it. The movie was a long movie with an intermission. During the intermission, I continued to complain, wondering aloud if maybe it was just the projector and that the second half may be sharper.

The man sitting next to me spoke up and said, "No, I asked the usher, and he said it is in the film." As I was turning away the Lord spoke to me, "Ask him what he does for a living," so I turned back and asked, "May I ask what you do for a living?" He answered, "I am a lithographer."

Now, it would take a printer to know that a lithographer was like a snobbish way of saying "printer." I didn't know why God would have me ask him that though. Then I heard, "Ask him where he works." So, I did. He named a printing company that didn't mean anything to me, and I was about to turn back in my seat when the Lord said, "Ask him where else." So, I did. I did this a few more times, to the point where I felt bruises in my spiritual sides with all the prodding I was getting from the Lord.

When finally I asked, "Anywhere else?" He said, "Well, I used to teach printing in Portland." I was beginning to get it. So I asked, "Where?" He named the high school that I attended. I heard the Lord tell me to ask him his name, but I really didn't need the poke this time. "What is your name?" He told me. He was my high school shop teacher. My favorite teacher and I hadn't recognized him at all.

I introduced myself, told him that I had gone on to own my own print shop, but now I was a pastor. He said, "Really? My wife and I have been trying to find God. We have driven all over town looking at church buildings. We even signed those cards you get in the mail 'if you want someone to contact you,' but nobody has called." I got to lead my favorite high school teacher to the Lord and his wife, too!

I led over 100 people to Christ that year. I heard that John Wimber was even sharing my testimony. Every day a miracle!

### *Shaking with Purpose*

My church decided to hold a Spiritual Gifts Seminar in Salem, Oregon. Brent Rue of Vineyard was going to be the speaker. We rented the largest facility in town at the Oregon State Fairgrounds. The newspaper ran full-page stories about the event. Even though nobody in Salem had heard of Vineyard, the testimonies of miracles were causing quite a stir.

We had almost 2,500 people come to the seminar, which is a lot when you consider that our church was less than 200. People came from everywhere. Our whole church contributed as support staff, music, registrations, book and tape sales, etc.

During the seminar, Brent taught about the gifts of the Holy Spirit. In typical Vineyard style, we had a clinic afterward, where people got to try to respond to the gifts. An example would be someone who believed they had received a word of knowledge speaking up, "Does anyone have a pain in their right knee?" If someone did, then the person who got the word would pray for the person with the hurt knee to get healed. There were hundreds of testimonies of such healings as a result.

On the last night during the clinic time, my staff wanted to join in the fun. It is funny how people want to pray if they believe something is really going to happen. I released them all and stayed back with the books and tapes. There I was alone, tired, no, EXHAUSTED, and watching in awe as hundreds of people were praying for each other. Many were experiencing healing or praying for healing for the first time. It sounded like a roar in the cavernous room. But what a sight it was.

As I leaned back with my chair against the wall, I heard an audible voice. It was from God, but it wasn't His voice. It was as if He was playing back a recording of me. It was my voice from a year earlier asking, "Why am I shaking?" Then, in the still, small voice inside of me, He said, "THAT'S why." I knew that he meant the hundreds of ordinary people who were experiencing His power for the first time.

## *Dealing With Skeptics*

When I was in India at the house church conference, most of my time there was just learning about the house church movement, and I didn't really minister anywhere. I was only going to minister one day in one place, and I was going to teach a healing clinic similar to the spiritual gifts conference I organized in Salem. It was kind of funny because I had forgotten my bible and any notes I had. I just prayed, "Come Holy Spirit."

I noticed a woman in the front row, trembling, and I asked her to come up front. She wasn't sick, she just felt God's presence on her very strongly and didn't know what was happening. When I prayed for her, she fell flat on the ground, and after a few minutes I helped her up.

There were some people who were very vocally scoffing, and when I asked what they were talking about, they responded in a rather mocking fashion, "Do people have to fall down to get healed?" I responded, "Of course not." While I could understand their skepticism, I warned them that manifestations like shaking or falling down often happened in scripture and throughout church history, and that they should not judge but be open to what God was doing.

When I helped the lady up, I tried to send her back to her seat, but she refused. She told me that her hands were burning and that she had to pray for somebody.

I asked anybody who was sick or injured to come forward. The first man had an injured knee. As she put her burning hands on his knee and prayed, the pain instantly left. Many others were healed in the same fashion. The mockers became quiet very quickly and all of them joined the prayer line. I didn't directly pray for anybody, but God showed up and demonstrated His power with manifestations.

When my clinic was over, the pastor came up to me wanting to know when I would return. He told me that a young lady in the church had approached him and told him that she had never experienced the presence of God so strong in her life.

This whole chapter has been my stories. What is the teaching? What scriptures do I use to prove these things really happened? I can't prove it. It is my testimony, my account of just some of what happened. An encounter with God, in a way that did not fit my religious experience, literally changed not only my life, but hundreds of people in my region. It is my story about how God can work through an uneducated nobody, and do extraordinary things to affect a whole city.

Don't tell me it can't be done or that you can't do it. I was there, it happened. It can happen again, and it can happen through you.

# NONE OF THEM WOULD HAVE HAPPENED WITHOUT YOU!

*"Don't think you are better than you really are. Be honest in your evaluation of yourselves, measuring yourselves by the faith God has given us"* (Romans 12:3, NLT).

For me it has always been a concern, how to be confident in times of crisis, or when preaching and demonstrating the power of God, without becoming arrogant and prideful. Please understand that when God performs a miracle through me, it is the most humbling of experiences.

But in the telling of testimonies, people by nature exalt the person God used in the story, as if these things were done because of some special greatness. But on the other hand, if I take no risks, then nothing happens. Humility is not the same thing as being fearful and avoiding risk. We are instructed to *"Be strong and of a good courage..."* (*Joshua 1:9, KJV*), and I try to do that.

There are times (because of all my testimonies) when people think I can just perform miracles at will. This couldn't be further from the truth. I am so completely dependent on the gentle leading of the Holy Spirit to do anything, including things that most pastors do and take for granted. I am always conscious of the state of my heart and my ability to hear.

I love to go to other churches and speak, if not for the simple reason that they have not already heard all my stories. This became painfully obvious to me one night after speaking at a friend's church.

Rather than give some deep theological teaching that I would have to fake, I normally share lots of testimonies of the miracles I have seen. My message is mostly, "If God can use me, He can use anybody," but this one night was extraordinary. I shared lots of stories of amazing miracles, and then the Holy Spirit fell in real power, touching everyone in the place.

Many people were healed, and just about everyone received prophetic words of encouragement. It was an amazing night, even better than I had hoped. You see, I wanted to do well. Not only for the people to receive all that God had for them, but also for my friend to be proud of me. Well, it was better than I had hoped, and people were really impressed... with me!

As I left for my car, it all sank in... "Ooooh noooooo!" I cried. "Oh God, I am so sorry," I cried with real tears. I literally felt as if I had touched the Glory, as if I had taken credit for what God had done. I felt as if this was the worst thing I could have done, like I would never see another miracle again, and I deserved it. I prayed, "God, I am so sorry. I can't even heal a cold."

There was a brief silence, I had expected a very long one. Then He spoke to me very clearly, "Randy, you are right. You can't even heal a cold." I think I was literally shaking in my car while waiting for what was coming next, what kind of discipline I was about to receive. But what I heard next was not what I had expected, not even close.

He said, "But, none of them (the miracles) would have happened without you!" It was the greatest compliment of my life, and it changed me forever.

You see, like any minister, I kind of have a shtick. Other pastors and ministers can do just about everything better than me, but my main ministry is in helping other ordinary joes like myself learn to walk in the supernatural. I believe that God wants all believers to be powerful representatives here on the earth. I believe that great revival will not come through some greatly anointed evangelist superstar, but through the whole body of Christ being anointed and carrying the authority of heaven wherever we go.

It is easy to say that God can do miracles through you any time He wants, but miracles rarely happen that way. God works through people ordinary people who take risks and people who make sacrifices to place themselves in the right place at the right time.

I am not telling you this so you will think that I am someone special. What I really want to do is to reach out to those who, like me, feel bypassed by God because other people seem to have all the stories.

I remember one day, while in intense prayer, you know the kind: "Oh Lord, bring revival, send forth your Spirit. Come, bring your power, bring your glory, heal the sick, and raise the dead. Come Lord…"

It was at this time that He interrupted me with that still, small voice and asked me a simple question, "You do know that in order to raise the dead, someone is going to have to die first?"

I instinctively knew that He wasn't talking about some cosmic cost for miracles. I immediately remembered the hospital rooms and homes I had been in where a loved one had just passed away. The grief and sadness is overwhelming, and so is the sense of helplessness. Those environments are not filled with faith, with the inspiring music playing, and with every head bowed and every eye closed. To have faith in that environment requires guts. I think what God was really asking me was, "Are you ready for this?"

In 2011, I sat under a tree with three African pastors. Two of them had raised people from the dead. One of the men (I am embarrassed to say I don't remember his name) had raised six different people from the dead in the African bush. He had come to meet with me, "the man of God," and I was literally humbled in his presence. He was nobody great to look at. Just a small, elderly gentleman. The suit he proudly wore was torn and dirty, but he was a faithful man. He treated his testimonies as no different than any other testimony of God's miracles. He just believed.

Like I said, I can't even heal a cold. But I would never have led anyone to Christ in Africa if I had never gone to Africa. You will never lead anyone to Christ if you don't witness. You will never see anyone healed if you don't pray for healing. You cannot sit at home or in the pew waiting for it to happen. It will never happen that way. You have to press in to God and then do what you think He is sending you to do.

If you will do your part, He will do His.

# TIME FOR NEW STORIES

*"You have some great stories, but they are old.
It is time for some new stories."*

In Revelation it says, *"They overcame by the blood of the Lamb and the word of their testimony" (Revelation 12:1, NKJV).* Our testimonies are the only evidence that some people will ever see or hear as proof that God is real and that He is alive and cares about people.

I have literally thousands of stories. They are not stories of the great things I have done, but they are stories about what God has done, miracles that I have personally witnessed and been a part of, impossible things that came to pass because God is living and active in our world today.

And while I constantly confess, "I can't even heal a cold," I believe that having the privilege to witness so many supernatural things didn't happen because I am just lucky or special. They happened because of faith and the faithfulness of God.

In Hebrews it says,

> *"And without faith it is impossible to please God, because anyone*
> *who comes to him must believe that he exists and that he rewards*
> *those who earnestly seek him"* (Hebrews 11:6, NIV).

I used to be fatalistic about faith. It seemed that I just didn't have any, or at least not enough. I heard all of the stories from evangelists who spoke in our church. I read every biography that I could get my hands on of great men and women of God. I read all sorts of accounts of revivals past and present, but I felt like these things were just for a few privileged, special people. I didn't realize that I was looking at the wrong part of the verse. All I could think was that I couldn't please God because I didn't have enough faith to heal the sick.

But it was never about me. I was not disqualified but rather qualified by Jesus. The part of the verse that I should have focused on was, *"He rewards those who earnestly seek Him."*

Anyone who has ever lost his car keys knows that the keys are not going to find themselves; oh sure, sometimes they just turn up during our normal routine, but in general, we have to look for them. You look earnestly, not giving up until you find them. At least if you need to go somewhere, you do. You look knowing that the keys have to be somewhere. You believe that you are going to find them eventually, and sure enough there they are, in the last place you look.

The same is true with God. First of all, don't make the same mistake I made. Don't go looking for the wrong thing. I was looking inside myself and and my circumstances for faith, and I was sadly lacking. Don't look within yourself for faith. Look for God, look for what He is doing!

The Bible says,

> *"So then faith comes by hearing, and hearing by the word of God"*
> *(Romans 10:17, NKJV).*

Faith comes! It is not just some talent you were born with. It comes from hearing God speak. I often tell people that even I could open the Red Sea, if God said, "Say 'Open.'" It has nothing to do with how great I am. I just need to hear from God and do it.

Ah, there's that hearing from God part again.... We are like the children of Israel, too afraid of God to seek Him ourselves.

They told Moses,

> *"You go and hear from God for us and then we will do it" (Exodus*
> *20:19, my paraphrase).*

Well, that is how we got the law, and we know how that worked out: the people failed, repeatedly, and needed a different option!

No, we have to hear from God for ourselves. Someone else's testimony may encourage us, but we have to hear for ourselves. We also can't just put words in God's mouth, telling ourselves what we want to hear and calling it God. That doesn't work either.

For years I went by the lessons of "faith teachers": "God said it. I believe it. That settles it." I would find a verse that fit my needs and "claim it." This actually worked sometimes. But a lot of the time it didn't, which left me questioning my faith or worse, questioning God.

I literally cringe sometimes when I hear people pray. It is hard to listen when they take the shotgun approach, quoting various scriptures as if they are trying everything, hoping that something will work. It feels like they are trying to find the magic words or something. Then they begin to tell God how big the problem is (as if He doesn't know). It feels to me as if they are trying to get God to repent and finally get around to caring and doing something, almost as if they are accusing God of the crime of not caring enough. I have never seen this work.

However, aligning with God, allowing Him to lead by His Spirit, almost always works. Well, it works all the time, but I don't always hear correctly; sometimes I get ahead of Him or put words in His mouth like others have done, but leaning into the heart of God will reveal a lot. He cares more than you or I, and He wants to heal, to save, and to bless. But He needs us. He needs us to hear and obey. He needs us to allow Him to lead.

This level of colaboring with God requires relationship. In a relationship there are conversations. In a good relationship we can talk about anything because trust has been developed, and all walls have been removed. All relationships require maintenance. You have to get your heart right and keep it right, and sometimes that is not so easy.

Sometimes we would rather that someone else hears for us, or perhaps we could just relate to God through His book. Sometimes we are afraid He will tell us something we don't want to hear, or we are afraid He will ask us to do something that we are afraid of, something that we are not, in our mind, ready for. Sometimes we believe lies, and they separate us from the kind of intimacy with God that allows us to discern His voice and know His heart.

As I mentioned in earlier chapters, there was a time in my life when I felt disillusioned. So many things had happened that I didn't understand, so I just quit trying. I couldn't hear from God because of the lies I believed, and to be honest, I no longer trusted in my ability to hear correctly.

Now during this time in my life (which lasted about seven years), I had many friends who wanted to see me restored to the old Randy. I had been somewhat of a hero to some of them in times past. Many came and called me to repentance. But I had seen so much, done so much, that none of them could relate. I had led hundreds to Christ and seen more miracles than any of them, maybe all of them put together.

After all, I was still the same person they knew before. I still loved the Lord. I just wasn't trying to change the world anymore. To be honest, just like Sampson in the Bible (Judges 16:20), I arrogantly thought that if I wanted to, I could just brush myself off and go and do great deeds again. This was not true. I just didn't know it yet.

One day another of my friends came by my print shop. I was doing some work for him. During the course of the afternoon, our conversation turned to my spiritual condition. I gracefully listened as I always did and then proceeded to defend myself, claiming that I still loved the Lord but after all that I had seen and done, I just couldn't go back to normal church where these things seldom, if ever, happened. I began to tell some of my stories to prove my point.

Then he got me.

"Randy, you have a lot of stories and they are awesome stories, but they are all old stories. It is time for some new stories."

I pretty much brushed him off, telling him that I would pray about it or something, but his words were from God, and I knew it. His words exposed pain in my heart, and they wouldn't go away. I even tried to get myself back into spiritual shape, but like Sampson, I found that I couldn't do it. I still believed all the same things. I had a great deal of experience in the supernatural, but I just couldn't reproduce it. Now I started to get scared. I had always thought that I could just turn it back on, but I couldn't.

I began to earnestly search for God. I desperately tried to repent. But I didn't even know what I had to repent from, and it seemed to me that God was playing hard to get. I couldn't hear Him, I couldn't feel Him, and I just plain didn't understand. This went on for over a year.

Then one day my friend Tom called, and he wanted to meet for lunch. I knew that he wanted to give me the "get right or get left" speech, something that I couldn't seem to do anything about; but Tom had every right. He had been my prayer partner through almost all of my stories. He had been behind me, encouraging me when no one else would. Of course I would meet with him, and I would gracefully receive anything he had to say.

But I was also in no hurry to do so. Appointment after appointment got canceled or rescheduled. Finally, on a day we were supposed to meet for lunch, he had to cancel. Later on in the afternoon, I learned that Tom had gotten some bad news from his doctor. He had terminal cancer with as little as one year to live. Since I was the one with all the stories of miraculous healings, I figured the least I could do was go and pray for him.

After work that night, I went to his house. The hot summer evening air breezed through his open front door, and I could see Tom's whole family sitting in the front room, including his four adult children. Instantly I knew what was happening: he planned to tell them what the doctor had said. I tried to excuse myself and said I would come back at another time, but they would have nothing of it. So they pulled up a chair for me, and I listened while they discussed what to do. Tom, with incredible peace, declared that he was going to trust God. But his family remained in shock and fear.

I quietly prayed, "Lord this family needs a pastor here right now," trying to think of who I could call. Then He spoke to me in a voice I had not heard like this in years, "How about you?"

It was at that moment that I realized how far I had fallen. I just wasn't ready for this. I didn't know what to do, and most of all I didn't feel very spiritual. However, I had learned a long time ago that when God spoke, that was the time to act. I said, "Okay."

I don't really remember all that happened that night, but with an authority I did not come in with, I began to minister. I got each person to share their thoughts and fears, and somehow with an anointing that I hadn't felt in years, I ministered to each one of them. God's presence was so strong in that room. And, of course, we also prayed for Tom.

When we were done, I was back sitting in my chair and God spoke to me again, "Which Randy do you like better, who you were before you came in here or who you are now?" I didn't even answer. I just pulled my chair into the middle of the room and asked everyone to pray for me, I was rededicating my life to Jesus.

It was only afterwards that they took me into the kitchen and showed me a list of names on the kitchen cupboard. At the top of the list was my name. It turns out that the whole family had taken and split up all of the meals in the month. Each would fast for the meals that they had chosen and pray especially for the names on that list. I was their first answer to prayer.

Tom wasn't healed that night, but we were not fazed. I instructed Tom that we needed to seek the Lord.

I read a verse to him:

> *"God seeks worshipers who will worship in Spirit and Truth"* *(John 4:23–24, my paraphrase).*

We were going to worship.

What better place to look for God than where God was looking? We started a prayer meeting, and I gave Tom the assignment to choose worship songs from his CD player for each meeting.

We would worship for hours. Tom spent all week worshiping and listening to songs about God's goodness. He loved to prayerfully choose just the right music that He thought God had for each week's meeting.

In these meetings we would worship for hours, and the Spirit of the Lord fell. People came from all around as news of the great things God was doing spread. Every week people were saved, healed, and renewed in their faith. Some people were called to ministry in that little house.

More and more stories were happening. So many that Tom's kitchen became like Grand Central Station. I couldn't let a single day go by without calling to find out what reports had come in about what God had done that day.

And now? As I sit typing the last chapter of this book, God is again calling me to new frontiers and new adventures. I will be leaving the church that I love and again pressing into unknown horizons, going to new countries, and partnering with new friends. It is scary really, but as I read my own book, I realize that I should be excited. Hasn't God always been with me before? He is SO faithful! So why wouldn't I think that He will be with me in the future?

## *How about you?*

Are you ready for new stories? New adventures with God?

I have written my book with every intent and desire to empower you to believe that God is with you to do supernatural things. I am not suggesting that you just choose the most impossible thing that you can imagine and then try to make that happen. My stories happened during the course of my life in relationship with God. As the Scripture says, *"And these signs shall follow them that believe…" (Mark 16:17, KJV)*. My advice is that you look into the eyes of your Savior and ask Him what adventures He has for you. And whatever He says, whether big or small, have the courage to say yes!

### *A note to my readers*

I would like to hear from you! All of the hard work that has gone into this book had a purpose; to empower YOU to do great exploits with God. If I can help in any way... especially prayer, I will do so.

**There are many ways to contact me:**

**My Facebook Page:** https://www.facebook.com/randy.conger.5

*or* https://www.facebook.com/whatisgodsayingbook?fref=ts

**or my personal email**: randyconger@yahoo.com

**What is God Saying is available:**

**Kindle**

http://www.amazon.com/Saying-other-Lessons-Spiritual-Father-ebook/dp/B00QSR6IVO

**Printed Version from Amazon:**

coming soon

or by contacting me directly (email)

**Free Version**

While I need finances just like everybody else, if you cannot afford the book an electronic version (PDF) is available free to anyone who asks.

Made in the USA
Lexington, KY
25 October 2019